When the first plane hit tower one, it seemed to be an accident. When the second plane hit tower two, it was an obvious deliberate attack. When the third plane hit the Pentagon, it was a declaration of war against the United States of America.

—*President George W. Bush*
His take on the attacks that occurred on the
morning of September 11, 2001

A US-led military response was inevitable at this point, and the entire world knew it was soon coming.

On that day, thousands of US military Active Duty, Reserve, National Guard, and their family members' lives would forever change.

When I was a teenager growing up in the mid to late 1980s, I used to watch war movies such as *Rambo*, *Platoon*, and *Full Metal Jacket*. I wished I could have been a Vietnam War veteran growing up in that particular era of the late 1960s and early 1970s. In 2003, when I served as an Infantry Platoon sergeant in the 82nd Airborne Division fighting in the Middle East, I realized the phrase "Be careful for what you wish for."

PRAISE FOR

WAKE UP, YOU'RE HAVING ANOTHER NIGHTMARE

"An extremely remarkable book created with fearlessness, strength, honesty and every other ingredient that phenomenal soldiers are made of. Nate's unmatched courage to share his stories with us, and his wife Jessica's relentless support through Nate's most difficult times are, to say the least, incredibly inspiring."

—Colonel John Schwemmer, US Army

"Nate Aguinaga and his wife, Jessica, do an excellent job of lifting the veil on life after serving and what it's like to live with PTSD. Nate allows you into some of his most trying times, and Jessica speaks openly on loving Nate through some of his struggles with PTSD. Through this book both Nate and Jessica are able to accurately describe the burdens and joys that come along with serving our country as a service member or spouse."

—Lisa Yearsin Flores, Support Contractor to the Office of Naval Research and Proud Army Wife to Army Corporal Benjamin Flores

"Sad but true, Nate does an awesome job describing the cumulative stresses of military combat operations and, more importantly, the aftereffects so many of our great warriors deal with on a daily basis. Knowing how to cope is so important! It was indeed an honor to serve with Nate and even more to know he is coping so very well with his own PTSD. A must read by all to fully understand—you are not alone."

—Command Sergeant Major (Retired) Michael Evans, US Army

"The book was great! I am truly amazed at all Nate and his wife, Jessica, have weathered together! Nate is gifted at bringing the reader to exactly where he has been with the details he gives. His writing truly resonates. It was fascinating and impactful as well to hear from a loved one's perspective on living with someone who has PTSD."

—Major Crystal Carroll, US Army

"Nate's third book ties the previous two books together, giving the reader intricate details of several of his firsthand accounts during Hurricane Katrina and tours in Iraq. These accounts provide insight on what a soldier has endured during conflict and relief events, which helps the reader understand what memories soldiers live with daily."

—Joshua Stufft, Operations & Logistics Manager, Marathon Pipe Line

Wake Up, You're Having Another Nightmare
by Nathan Aguinaga

© Copyright 2020 Nathan Aguinaga

ISBN 978-1-64663-167-4

All rights reserved. No part of this publication may be reproduced, stored in a retrieval system, or transmitted in any form or by any means—electronic, mechanical, photocopy, recording, or any other—except for brief quotations in printed reviews, without the prior written permission of the author.

Published by

3705 Shore Drive
Virginia Beach, VA 23455
800–435–4811
www.koehlerbooks.com

WAKE UP, YOU'RE HAVING ANOTHER NIGHTMARE

NATHAN AGUINAGA

VIRGINIA BEACH
CAPE CHARLES

TABLE OF CONTENTS

FOREWORD VIII

INTRODUCTION 1

CHAPTER 1: 2003-2004—Just South Of Baghdad
                The Triangle of Death 4

CHAPTER 2: September 2005—New Orleans,
                Louisiana 22

CHAPTER 3: October 2000—Drill Sergeant School 30

CHAPTER 4: December 2000 to December 2002—
                My Time On The Trail 52

CHAPTER 5: 2008-2009—Kadhimiya District
                Northwest Baghdad 78

CHAPTER 6: Wake Up—Living With Someone
                Who Has Ptsd— A Testimonial From
                Jessica Aguinaga, Nathan's Wife 87

CHAPTER 7: Counseling After Retirement. 106

ACKNOWLEDGMENTS 135

FOREWORD

Memorial Day is a somber day for me, as it is for all veterans and their families. I try my best to visit a place which honors the fallen. This includes national cemeteries, the 9/11 memorial in New York City, and other places which honor fallen servicemembers. Regardless of where I can or cannot be, I dedicate much of the day in remembrance of those friends and soldiers I lost in our wars following 9/11. Sitting quietly with my wife on our porch on Memorial Day 2020, I shared a story of an IED which struck a vehicle carrying several of my soldiers. The blast was significant enough to lift a forty-ton vehicle off the ground and onto its side. Many of the vehicle's occupants were evacuated by helicopter to a forward medical facility at a base I happened to be at. I rushed there to be present when they were brought in.

Early reports indicated that each of the soldiers was alive and not seriously injured. They were wheeled into the treatment room where Army doctors and nurses sprang into action. The soldiers were in shock, and I wanted them to know I was there. Perhaps it would give them some sense of comfort to see their commander and brother in this fierce fight we were in. I walked over to each of them, placed my hand atop their head, and looked them in the eye, telling them that I was with them and they were going to be okay. Each of them began to weep. I'll never knew exactly what they were feeling, but they seemed to be tears of relief. They were alive and back in the relative safety of a fortified base. Their leader was here and would look after them.

They were alive in part because of a decision I made to stop the use of flat-bottomed, thin-skinned Humvee vehicles and transition to safer armored, V-hulled vehicles. Had these men been traveling in a Humvee, they would surely have been killed. I was able to stay with these soldiers and connect them with their family members via satellite telephone. I've always recalled this memory, but as I shared it with my wife, I began to weep. It had a profound impact on me, but I would not allow myself to truly feel it. I suppressed my emotions because I was the leader and needed to remain stoic and strong for my unit. In the safe company of my life partner, Leslie, a full decade after that incident, I reacted differently and I didn't see it coming. It was a very healing experience. I mustered the courage to share a story I had not before and the courage to allow my true emotions to escape.

I've witnessed courage in numerous forms in my decades of military service. I've seen it through the actions of a US Army Jumpmaster extending his or her body fully outside the door of an aircraft while in flight. I've seen it in a military spouse who comforts children who see their mother or father off to war. I've seen it in combat where a young noncommissioned officer, in the most horrific of conditions, led his or her soldiers from the front. I've also witnessed it in the act of a combat veteran who seeks professional help to better manage the horrors which will never leave them. This book is a shining example of that courage. Nate Aguinaga, backed by his loving children and amazing wife, Jessica, sought the help of professionals to deal with his trauma. And while this act is courageous, it is even more courageous of a veteran (and his or her loving spouse) to produce a book which shares their deepest struggles with the world. Nate and Jessica display this courage in the pages ahead.

Combat injures a warrior for life, and while many of us return from war without a physical scratch, the real damage lies beyond view in our psyche. No warrior will ever escape the gruesome sights, sounds and smells of combat. Leaders like Nate will carry their decisions and words, right or wrong, with them forever. Some of these memories and images may lie dormant, resurfacing in odd times when a sight, sound or smell triggers a memory. Veterans handle these horrors in a variety of ways. Their effects manifest in a variety of ways such as overdrinking, drug abuse, abuse, depression and even suicide. Nate shares his own reactions vividly in this book. Some veterans may feel the effects of combat only after they transition and are gone from the security and camaraderie of their military tribe. Some will struggle immediately after these experiences. Most professional counselors and psychiatrists promote journaling and sketching as part of a larger approach to manage this trauma. I suspect this book was very healing for Nate and maybe even for his family. One thing is for certain: Nate is not alone.

I saw myself in his stories. I recalled the stench, the dryness of my mouth and tightening of my chest. I remembered the images, which I can still see clearly, and my words and actions. They are still very much alive in me, and, like Nate, I too must turn to writing, talking, counseling, and to the enduring support of my family, especially my wife, Leslie. I could identify with Nate and Jessica's relationship and their journey dealing with Nate's trauma. Like Nate, I am proud of my service in the US Army. I wouldn't trade it for anything. Freedom is not free. It will always come at a cost. Combat veterans like Nate Aguinaga are the bill payers for our freedom, and the receipt for their service is the suffering they carry well beyond the battlefield.

Nate gives it to you as he does in all of his books, in true noncommissioned officer fashion—raw and unadorned. *Wake Up, You're Having Another Nightmare* is a book every combat veteran and their spouse should read. Nate will be the first to tell you the publishing of this book is not the final bandage for his wounds. He is on a journey of healing and has taken concrete steps in that direction. Moreover, he continues to serve, sharing his story for the benefit of other veterans. If you have picked up this book, you are probably a veteran, spouse, family member or a person passionate about serving those who have served our nation. Wake up from your own nightmare. Start with this book, then display courage as Nate has by seeking help. Turn the page and get started. Wake up.

—Colonel (Retired) Rob Campbell, US Army
Author, *It's Personal, Not Personnel: Leadership Lessons for the Battlefield and the Boardroom* and *At Ease: A Soldier's Story and Perspectives on the Journey to an Encore Life and Career*

Two of the most insulting questions anyone can ever ask a combat veteran is, "Have you ever killed anybody," or, "How many people have you killed?"

A few days after I got back from Iraq in 2004, my wife and I were shopping at the Post Exchange on Fort Bragg. When we were done, we were walking to our vehicle in the parking lot. She noticed a toy on the ground that must have fallen out of somebody's cart. It was brand new, still in its box. As she approached it, I began screaming at her, "Get the fuck away from it—it's gonna fucking blow!" I then realized where I was at and looked around as others in the parking lot were looking at me with signs of shocked confusion. A little over a year later, she became my ex-wife.

INTRODUCTION

Make no mistake about it. I am not crazy or mentally deranged. I do not suffer from a bi-polar or schizophrenia disorder, nor do I even suffer at all, for that matter—not in my opinion, anyway, but then again, I am not a psychologist or psychiatrist, either. The truth of the matter is that I've been afraid to write this book, because when you write a book, you have to take yourself back to the moments you are talking about. That has been difficult for me. When I decided to go ahead and attempt to write this, I had to convince myself that I had to not only be honest with the readers, but with myself first. I do have guilt, shame, and embarrassment. That's okay, though, because I am a human being who is still trying to figure out life.

I do not feel sorry for myself, and it is difficult for me to feel sorry for other adults around me, especially those that can care for themselves. Do I fly off the handle at times when things do not go my way and in a prompt and timely manner? Hell yes, I do, and quite frequently, I might add. Is it because of my Post-Traumatic Stress Disorder or because of the fact that I spent almost my entire twenty years in the Army as a leader that demanded positive results at all times and quickly? I think more of the latter.

In 2009, I was clinically diagnosed with Post-Traumatic Stress Disorder from an Army psychiatrist. Post-Traumatic Stress Disorder, or simply PTSD, is a psychological disorder when an individual believes or encounters a moment or moments when his or her life could end and/or has seen death. Not only military members, but police officers, firefighters, and first responders encounter this throughout their careers for serving their daily duties as well. So do children or adults that have been part of a bad, emotional experience, such as abuse, a car accident, etc. Most of my friends where I live currently are firefighters and first responders, and we talk about what they see commonly on their call-out duties.

During World War I, psychiatrists referred to this disorder as "shellshock." Experiencing death or encountering nearby death experiences or intense situations can affect any human being and not necessarily in the same manner. The Army actually diagnoses it as Post-Traumatic Stress Anxiety and Depression Disorder.

I finally went to the Army Mental Health Clinic after my wife convinced me to do so. Oh, yeah, she was my new wife for almost two years at that point, and she too had some experience of living with someone who had PTSD. Her father was a three-tour Vietnam War veteran who often had nightmares and, to this day, has to sleep with a nightlight on in his room at night. PTSD does not necessarily have to do with just combat experiences or death, either. That is my opinion on the description as well, not necessarily a clinical definition. I say this because my nightmares and bad frightening experiences do not all have to do with death or destruction. Bear with me, as I will explain all of this in this book, ladies and gentlemen. Thank you.

My nightmares got to the point where my wife would actually have to get out of the bed and move to the opposite end of the room, because she did not know what my nightmare end-state might be. Once she was at a safe distance from me, she would holler out my name until I would wake up. Once awake, I would go to the kitchen and get a glass of water and pace around for a little while. "How long before this wife leaves me?" I would ask myself this for those first two or three years of our marriage.

When I went to the mental health clinic at our post hospital, I was diagnosed with PTSD within the first hour. I was asked a series of questions after filling out an extensive questionnaire. After that, it was weekly therapy meetings with both me and my wife with one of the psychiatrists. Not marriage counseling or anything like that, but how to cope with this disorder in order to sustain normal living. Eleven years later, I still attend bi-monthly counseling sessions with a social worker at my local Veterans Administration Clinic (the VA).

CHAPTER 1

2003-2004
JUST SOUTH OF BAGHDAD
THE TRIANGLE OF DEATH

I am not going to discuss every detail, firefight, nightly indirect fire attack, or combat patrol, for this is not a book about war. Besides, my experiences could never compare to those of *Black Hawk Down*, *American Sniper*, and especially *Lone Survivor*—not even close. I will talk to you about certain events that still haunt me to this day, mostly in my sleep, and I believe always will for the rest of my life. The most important individuals in combat are your medics and surgeons. Thank you, God, for these individuals; that's no bullcrap.

My unit in the 505th Parachute Infantry Regiment, 82nd Airborne Division, was headquartered in Mumuhdyah, Iraq, at Forward Operating Base (FOB) Saint Michael. It was named Saint Michael after an enemy mortar round landed on the roof of the chicken processing factory that our battalion cleaned and began housing our companies in while we, along with engineers, were building the back forty of the rest of the FOB. The mortar round was a dud and did not explode. If it had detonated, it would have killed dozens, if not more, of the paratroopers in our battalion. The name quickly became Saint Michael, *Protector of Paratroopers*, right after that miracle. That's a true story. I mentioned it in *Division* briefly.

This area of Iraq became known to Coalition Forces as the "triangle of death." The triangle, formed by the cities of Yusufiyah to the northwest, Latifiyah to the south, and Mumuhdyah to the east, held the fastest routes from Baghdad southward to the Shiite shrines in Najaf and Karbala. The major terrain feature of the triangle of death was the Euphrates River, which bordered the triangle to the southwest. The terrain was mostly farmland but was sliced by many irrigation ditches. These areas were also surrounded by hundreds of rural villages as well.

I and my platoon just finished a daily patrol in a neighborhood in Latifiyah. It was my company's primary sector of responsibility (Alpha Company). We were out conducting routine knock and talks with the local Iraqis, going house to house. We would ask the homeowners questions, such as if they had any information or concerns about any enemy activity within these neighborhoods. We would get the homeowners' names, ask them how many members were in their households, and if they had any weapons. We would also take a picture of them with their addresses.

Occasionally, we would come across a home where the owner would not open the door but would move the curtains, so we knew they were home, and immediately they became suspected of hiding something—usually weapons or bomb-making material. We would have to kick in their doors and search their homes. We'd have to blow the hinges off the door with a twelve-gauge shotgun and occasionally would find heavy weapon systems, take the two or three military-aged males from the home, zip-tie their hands behind their backs, and put sandbags over their heads. We would then take them back to the base with us and turn them over to our military intelligence interrogators.

One time, we found a Russian machine gun in a couch. Yes, I'm not shitting you. They had the springs torn out of it with a thin sheet of wood over it and had the cushions on top of that. Pretty sneaky, but we knew they were hiding something because they wouldn't open their door. We searched the small home and didn't find anything until I told one of my team leaders to take the fucking cushions off the couch, and low and behold, there it was. The owner tried to tell us he didn't know how it got there. He soon had a sandbag over his head and was heading back to FOB Saint Michael with us.

It wasn't always bad. I mean, we tried to make it as humanly fun as we could when we were in these villages. We passed out candy to the kids. Hell, sometimes we would pull out dollar bills and give each one of these kids a dollar. Normally, we had about three or four kids that would just be hanging around our vehicles. The next thing you know, in a matter of ten minutes, the entire village's children would storm around us mysteriously. "Mista, mista, mista," they'd say with their hands out for a dollar. The Iraqi locals always referred to us as "Mista." It wasn't bad; we didn't mind. Usually, we had someone with a portable CD player (remember those?) with some small speakers hooked up to them. We'd put them on the roof of the vehicles and play some current music at the time, like Jay-Z or the Black-Eyed Peas. We would clap our hands, and the kids would have a ball. We also had brand new soccer balls we'd pass out to them, and they would go ape-shit.

Soon, the short moments of fun would end, and it would be time to head back and remember we were in a war. "Time to head back, gentlemen. Let's go," I would have to tell them. It was hard to leave good moments like this, primarily because we all had families and children back home that we wished we could play with. In reality, though, we did not get too attached to these locals. The Sunni insurgency would figure out a way to kill them and their families if they got the word that they were getting too close to the Americans. It was as simple as that. It was black and white, no gray area. Our Iraqi interpreters were simply trying to earn a paycheck to feed and take care of their families. Unfortunately, they had to start leaving them. The bad guys started killing them off in their homes and killing their wives, too. So we ended up having them living on our base so that they could be protected and better hidden. Those insurgents were fucking savages—fact. Like the old Metallica song—"Sad but True."

Those rides back to base were pretty stressful, because you just hoped to make it back without getting hit with an Improvised Explosive Device (IED) or rocket-propelled grenade or simply getting ambushed with small arms fire, especially when driving through the congested crowds of downtown Mumuhdyah itself. I always feared someone lobbing a grenade inside our vehicle. That's why I always had my M-4 outside the window of my door, telling everyone, "Get the fuck back." This was about six to eight months before we started getting up-armored vehicles over there. Whenever our convoy would get downtown in those streets and our speeds dropped to ten miles per hour, our standard procedure was to dismount the vehicles and walk alongside the vehicles. This was with the exception of the drivers and gunners on top of each Humvee, of course.

One mission was to conduct a raid on a small complex. It was a battalion mission, and our company was the main effort. Delta Company was to secure the intersections that surrounded this small compound of about two or three houses, out in the middle of nowhere. Bravo Company was to have our internal support and security as well. Charlie Company was back pulling FOB security, which included manning the entrance gate. This was back when battalions were responsible for manning their own guard posts internally. Now, they usually have a separate unit pull the security. My last tour in Iraq, we had the Ugandan Army pulling the security on our FOB.

Anyway, we convoyed out to this little village at, like, 0230, with a hit time of 0330 or something like that. It was only a few miles away. Our mission was to secure and capture two bad guys that were affiliated with Al Qaeda, and they were to be found within this compound. Delta Company led out first in order to get into their positions and blockade all the entrances into the compound. Once we arrived, each platoon in our company dismounted their vehicles. Usually, we would have at least two soldiers, such as the drivers and another guy for security, to stay with each truck and guard them.

As we approached our assigned houses, we lined up by squads and began our entry procedures. I would move up with the initial breach squad, knock on the door, and holler out, "Open up! Coalition Forces!" I immediately heard a female screaming inside the house. After about ten seconds, I gave the hand and arm signal to forcefully breach. We did this usually by kicking the door in after checking for wires around it. Once inside, we began clearing room by room. They didn't know we were coming because we always traveled with our vehicle headlights off. We had this shit down to a science.

Once cleared, we separated women and children and collected up the military-aged males and took them outside. We made them get on their knees with their heads down along the side of the home. Of course, we would put a couple of guys on them for security. The two males we got from our house were the targets we were after, which meant our platoon was responsible for securing them and taking them back to our base. They were positively identified as the targets from our Military Intelligence guy we had with us. We zip-tied their hands, put sandbags over their heads, and took them to our vehicles. Our Platoon Leader called it into the Company Commander that we got them. He, in turn, would call it into the Battalion Commander, who was on site as well.

I went back inside with our interpreter and informed the females that we were taking these men back with us for an undetermined amount of time. A couple of them started crying and even screaming at us. I didn't give a fuck; they should have not been trying to mortar and rocket our fucking FOB or blow up our fucking vehicles daily. "Let's go," I told the interpreter. "All blue elements, load up, separate the prisoners in two separate vehicles, and prepare to move out." Once the battalion commander gave the order, we moved off the complex and headed back to FOB Saint Michael. Again, I hoped that we wouldn't get hit with an IED on the way back.

Once back, I ordered the squads to lock and clear their weapons, and they reported back they were all green. I told them to drop me off at the detention center on the back forty of the FOB. I then took the prisoners myself into the tent where we had cells built for them. I ordered the platoon to fill up the vehicles at the fuel point, unload all the equipment, and go eat chow. The sun was just coming up.

I entered the tent and turned the prisoners over to the guards in the inside. It smelled so disgusting in there, to the point that I will never forget it. The prisoners were kept in there for no more than about forty-eight to seventy-two hours. Then, after their interrogation process, they would get sent to bigger, actual prisons or even Guantanamo. I didn't really give two shits. Our job was to capture them from the battlefield. What they did with them afterwards wasn't my concern.

When I walked into the door of the tent, one of the guards who was a young black soldier hollered out, "Oh shit! Motherfuckin' Sergeant Augi's up in this motherfucker! Goddamn!"

The other guard said, "Man, Sergeant Augi's motherfuckin' *Clint Eastwood* up in this motherfucka!"

I said back to them, "I don't want to hear all the bullshit, gentlemen. Just take these two motherfuckers. Where's the sign-in sheet?" We had to annotate target numbers that the battalion provided (bad guys were marked by a target number), mission number, location of capture, and date and time. Once they got them in separate cells, they cut off the zip-ties and removed the sandbags from their heads.

"Man, Big Sarge, you da man up in this motherfucker!"

The other guy repeated, "Man, motherfuckin' *Clint Eastwood* up in this motherfucka."

I just shook my head and said, "I'm going to get me some scrambled eggs and sausage. Did you boys get something to eat?"

"Oh, yeah, Big Sarge, we had an MRE when we first got on duty out here, because the chow hall wasn't open yet."

"Okay, have a good one out here, and be careful."

"Thanks, Big Sarge!" the soldier said.

When I got to the mess hall, I ate my breakfast. When I left, I got two to-go containers for the two guards anyway. I loaded them up with eggs, bacon, some hash browns, and pancakes. I put two or three packets of butter, syrup, and salt and pepper in my cargo pockets for them, too. I even grabbed a bottle of Texas Pete hot sauce for them, because you cannot eat military scrambled eggs without it. It was our unwritten rule. I took it back to the detention center for them. When I walked in, you would have thought I gave them a million dollars apiece.

"Goddamn, Big Sarge, you da man! Thanks, Big Sarge!"

I turned around and said, "You gentlemen have a good day. You need anything else? Do you have enough ammunition?"

As they were choking down their food, they both shook their heads and replied, "Naw, we good, Big Sarge. Thanks, man."

"Okay, goodnight. I'm going to bed." It was about 0800.

"Goodnight, Big Sarge!" I believe their duty was twelve hours on and twelve hours off. Shitty detail to work and it came from our headquarters company.

A couple of days later, our platoon's mission was to patrol around the "Ammunition Depot," which was in between the route of Latifiyah and Yusafiyha. The "Depot" was an old Saddam Hussein Iraqi Army major ammunition supply point out in the middle of nowhere. There was no ammo out there anymore by this time. One of our battalion's missions was to patrol through it every now and then to ensure nobody was trying to steal copper pipes that were imbedded throughout the facility. They used the copper pipes for high-dollar sale that would eventually or could eventually be used to make bombs. One of our missions was obviously to stop and prevent it. Every now and again, we would encounter a couple or a few people that were out there trying to retrieve the copper, and we would have to deal with them.

We pulled up as we witnessed three dudes out there. By the way, they knew they were not authorized to be out there. That place was known to be off-limits for the locals—big time. We were a distance from them, maybe about three hundred meters or so. One of them began to fire at us. Too easy. "Light those motherfuckers up!" I gave the order to my M240B machine-gunner that was on my vehicle, and he did. All three were down immediately. That shit was so loud, too. There are no earplugs in combat, my friends. I mean, there is, but when you have to command and control with a radio, it makes it very difficult to use them. Therefore, I never wore them, and many others did not, either.

We didn't fuck around. I ordered three hundred sixty–degree security from the vehicles as we approached the bodies. I had my medic assess the bodies. Two were dead and one was still breathing but badly wounded. I called in the situation report to battalion headquarters. Simultaneously, I ordered two soldiers to grab the wounded guy and put him in the back of my HMMWV. We were going to take him back to the FOB for medical attention because he was still alive. Yes, we took care of enemy wounded, too, because we were not savages like those animals. We were not murderers; we were soldiers.

The Latifiyah police would pick up the two bodies while we were medical evacuating the live guy. We secured their one AK-47 that they were shooting at us with also. The bad guy in the back of my vehicle wasn't looking too good, obviously. He called out to me as I lit up a cigarette. "Mista, mista." He gave me the international hand signal for *give me a cigarette*, the two fingers to the mouth symbol. So I reached in my ammo pouch and pulled out my American pack of Marlboro Reds and handed him one. I then pulled out my lighter and lit it for him as well.

One of the privates in the back of the vehicle yelled at me, "Hey, Sergeant, fuck that shit. Don't give that motherfucker a goddamn cigarette! Fuck him!"

My anger level went to full capacity instantly. "You shut the fuck up, you little piece of shit! You don't fucking tell me what the fuck I'm going to do or not do, you little motherfucker! This guy's going to be dead by the time we even get back. So if I want to give a dying man his last cigarette, that's my business, you fucking shitbag! Don't *ever* question me again, fuck-stick! You hear me?!"

He replied calmly, "Yes, Sergeant."

Today, I still remember that exchange with that young man. I mean, I am Catholic. What was wrong with me giving a dying man his last cigarette? I hope he enjoyed it. I had my platoon medic with him and asked him, "Doc, is there anything you can do for him to keep him alive?" He looked me in the eyes and shook his head. The guy had five or six 7.62-millimeter bullet holes in his chest and abdomen. He was bleeding profusely. I looked back at my doc and nodded my head in response. He was dead in the back of my vehicle before we approached the outskirts of Latifiyah, which was about three miles up the road. The back of my HMMWV was full of his blood. That's okay, though. I knew just the right person who was going to clean it up. Quite often to this day, I have dreams of him asking me for that last cigarette.

When we arrived back to Saint Michael, I had my driver take us straight to the battalion aid station to drop off the body. When we pulled up, the First Sergeant was out front. I had two soldiers carry him inside as I stayed out with the First Sergeant. "So what happened out there?" he asked me, and I told him that we pulled up to the ammo depot and they started shooting at us, and I ended it quickly. He then asked me for a cigarette, and I gave him one.

The soldiers came back out of the aid station, and I told Staff Sergeant K, my weapons squad leader, to take the vehicle back down after they filled it up with fuel and that I wanted Private So-and-So to clean the back of it. "He will get two five-gallon jugs of water, a bottle of bleach, and a broom and clean the back of my vehicle. When I get back down there, I want him and you to show me, so I can inspect the motherfucker. Tell that little motherfucker the next time he questions me, I'm going to fuck his ass up!"

Staff Sergeant K replied, "Roger, Sergeant." The First Sergeant asked me what happened, and I told him about the cigarette episode. He just shook his head and laughed a little.

While smoking a cigarette with First Sergeant, two HMMWVs

came barreling into the area suddenly. The lead vehicle's windshield was shattered, so we immediately suspected an IED attack. "Help us! Somebody help us!"

I ran over immediately. "What can I do?"

"Grab him! Is this your aid station?"

I replied, "Yeah, man, this is it! Let's get him inside!" It was an MP unit with their wounded guy from an IED attack that they had just got hit by up the road on ASR Jackson, about a mile north. ASR means Ammunition Supply Route, our military named this one Jackson, but it was a four-lane highway that ran up straight to Baghdad.

I reached my hands in his shoulder areas of his IBA (body armor) and pulled him up. One of the MPs grabbed his legs, and we carried him inside the aid station, where we had at least two surgeons. I remember when I was carrying him inside, he coughed hard, and blood came splattering out of his mouth, getting on my face and on my IBA I still had on. We put him on a gurney, and I rolled him on his side to prevent him from choking on his own blood. "Doc, doc! He just got hit outside the wire!" I hollered out. One of the surgeons came out and rolled him inside their operating room. I left the aid station, told the First Sergeant goodbye, and headed down to the living area tents on our FOB. When I got down there, the first thing I did was inspect the back of my vehicle to ensure it was clean. Staff Sergeant K walked up to me and asked if I needed to see the Private that ran his mouth to me. I said no. I decided to let it go and that I just didn't want to see any more blood today or this evening. Who knew? The evening was still young . . .

I got into my shorts and towel and walked to the shower trailer, still with this MP's blood on my neck and face. When I got into the shower, I realized the only thing we accomplished for that day was that me and my platoon killed three people and some bad guys tried to kill a platoon of American soldiers. I just stood under the hot water, letting it run over my body, and shook my head. I may even have cried a little bit, but I won't admit that to you. I remember telling myself, "You better hurry up and dry off and get back to your tent behind the hescos before the bad guys start launching their nightly mortar rounds at us." It was almost dark out and creepy. Sometimes combat is a motherfucker.

The next day, I walked up there and asked if the MP had made it. They said he did and that he was going to Landstuhl, Germany, for medical evacuation. That was great news. Something positive came from that day that I'll never get back in my life. Anyway, my truck was spotless. I mean, you could have eaten off the bed of that vehicle.

One evening, we had just returned back to the FOB around 1900 from one of the knock and talk patrols down in Latifiyah. After we arrived, we headed to the mess hall for dinner chow. We had to eat our dinner before our nightly mortar round attempted attack from the bad guys. The reason I say "attempted" is because they couldn't hit shit. Yeah, those fuckers would launch between four to six rounds at us every night there for a while until we conducted a battalion raid on the nearby village outside of our FOB. That shit ended really quick after snatching up several of those motherfuckers and bringing them back to our detention facility.

Anyway, I got my tray of food, and on my way to sit down with my squad leaders, I was stopped by my First Sergeant, and he introduced me to our new Battalion EOD Sergeant. EOD stands for Explosive Ordinance Disposal, a pretty big deal in Iraq and the entire Global War on Terrorism. He was a young staff sergeant and seemed to be a very eager young man to go out and get into the fight, as we all were on a daily basis. I sat down with them and introduced myself to him. "How you doing, Sergeant? I'm Sergeant Aguinaga, but I go by Sergeant Augi, because 'Aguinaga' has too many syllables in it, and motherfuckers always mispronounce it anyways."

"I'm doing good, Sergeant," Staff Sergeant O replied back as we shook hands.

"When did you get in?" I asked.

"I got in this morning and can't wait to get out there and go to work, Sergeant."

"Don't worry, 'Big Sarge,' you'll get your chance and real fucking soon, I guarantee it. You got your work cut out for you over in this motherfucker."

"Yeah, so I've been hearing." We sat and talked about what was going on back in the States and ate our dinner together.

When I was done eating, I stood up and shook his hand. "All right, Sergeant, have a great night. Don't get hit by one of these mortars that'll get launched at us soon." He looked at me with a surprised look in his eyes. I then said to him, "Don't worry, those stupid fucks can't hit shit anyway. However, I ain't standing around outside waiting to become one of their lucky hits, either. You know what I'm sayin', Big Sarge?"

He started laughing. "I hear you, Sergeant Augi."

"Okay, have a good one, and I'm sure I'll be seeing you both in here and out in sector, too." That was the last time I saw that young man alive.

The next day, our platoon's mission was to pull security around a school in the town of Yusufiyah, which was Charlie Company's main sector of responsibility. Our platoon got tasked to assist one of their platoons with the security mission. Charlie Company had been helping the school by delivering supplies, such as paper, pens, notebooks, etc. Some bad guys threatened the teachers that if they accepted another pencil or piece of paper from the Americans, they were going to kill them and possibly blow up the school. The teachers were not intimidated, and we definitely were not, either. Our mentality was, "Bring it, motherfuckers, if you want some of this." It was a bad town, too. Out of all the towns of our battalion's responsibility, that was the worse. During our time there in Iraq, we had conducted several battalion-sized missions in that town.

The day was relatively quiet with no activity. Our two platoons pulled security around the school, and by the end of the day, around 1700, we got a radio call from battalion headquarters telling us to return to base. I gave my platoon the safety convoy brief and the order of movement back to the FOB. It was a considerably longer movement, since it was the farthest city away. At the end of my briefing, I told them when we get back to the FOB that we needed to watch the next episode of *24*. We were on a *24* kick during that time. Overall, it was a very calm, easy day. All we had to do was get back to Saint Michael, eat dinner, and watch our show. Little did I know, it was going to be an evening I will never forget and that continues to haunt me in my sleep to this day.

The sun was about to go down as we turned onto ASR Jackson to begin heading north towards Mumuhdyah and then to our base. Not too long after we made the turn, it came—the worse radio call we could have ever received. "Alpha Blue Seven, this is Three Panther Three November over." I'm not sure as I write this why our platoon leader was not with us that day, but he was back at the FOB to knock out administrative work he had to do, no big deal. It was actually common that he didn't go out with us on every single mission and vice versa. There were times I stayed back to take care of admin shit back at our command post, or CP, as well.

"Three Panther Three November, this is Alpha Blue Seven, go ahead over," I said.

"Roger, Alpha Blue Seven, you have a change of mission, break. You will proceed just north of the oil refinery on ASR Jackson and conduct a roadblock on both north- and southbound traffic, break. There has been an IED explosion with one friendly KIA from Three Panther. How copy over?"

My first reaction was, *What the fuck? Doesn't Hadji know he's fucking my shit up tonight? That we're supposed to have an easy night with watching the next episode of* 24? Then it hit me like a bolt of thunder: *Fuck, did he say KIA from our battalion?* KIA is the worst nomenclature that there is in the military. It stands for "killed in action," for those who did not know. "Three Panther Three November, roger, WILCO, we're in route to that location. Will notify when we arrive on site, over."

"Alpha Blue Seven, roger out."

WILCO stands for will comply. I then looked at my driver and said, "Fuck . . ."

I got on my platoon's internal radio and ordered, "All Blue elements, this is Blue Seven over."

They all replied:

"This is Blue one, over."

"Blue two, over."

"This is Blue three, over."

"Blue four, over."

"Roger, we have a change of mission. We will proceed northbound on ASR Jackson, just north of the oil refinery, break. There's been an explosion, possible IED, with one friendly KIA. Identity unknown at this time, break. Once on scene, our mission is to conduct a blockade on both north- and southbound lanes until further notice. How copy over?"

All four squad leaders responded in order with, "Roger that."

"All right, Blue Three, pick up the pace. Let's get on site ASAP, over."

We picked up our convoy speed to get to the scene, which was about ten miles up the road.

Once there on the obvious site, there was a military police element with two of their vehicles pulling security, a medical vehicle, and a couple EOD guys as well. We maneuvered our five vehicles to close off traffic on both north- and southbound lanes of ASR Jackson around the scene. My guys dismounted as per standard operating procedure. I pulled up near the MPs, called in to our battalion operations in order to notify them that we had arrived on scene and had the roadblock executed. I walked over to the EOD soldier with Staff Sergeant K, my weapons squad leader. "What the fuck happened, Sergeant?"

He looked at me with tears in his eyes, and I could tell he was so shaken up. "It was Staff Sergeant O, Sergeant Augi."

I replied in utter shock, "Staff Sergeant O?"

"Yes, Sergeant." He then broke down in tears.

I screamed out, "Goddamn it!" I turned around, pulled out my pack of cigarettes, and immediately lit one up. It was the new EOD guy that I had just had dinner with the night before.

So standard procedure is whenever an IED has been identified or suggested by the locals, the battalion sends out one of the two EOD teams with a security force to the scene to investigate and/or detonate it. Once they have identified the explosive device, they will detonate it. Once detonated, one of them must go up and confirm its destruction in order to declare the area is clear of danger. On his first mission in Iraq, Staff Sergeant O, as the team's NCOIC, went up to the small crater to confirm destruction of the IED. When he approached it, the enemy, who had eyes on them, apparently detonated a secondary IED, blowing him all over ASR Jackson. It was an overhead IED that was mounted on the walkway overpass just above the Staff Sergeant. It had been the first time our battalion had encountered such an IED and, more disturbingly, this tactic by any bad guy thus far. Those motherfuckers always studied and figured out our tactics, techniques, and procedures, hence why we always had to adjust and modify them constantly. This was a continuing problem that existed during the U.S.'s eight-year involvement in Iraq.

Staff Sergeant K walked up to me and asked me for a cigarette, and I gave him one. As we were facing the medics' vehicle, we both watched a scene we will never forget. I haven't, anyway, and I'm sure neither has he. One of the medics had Staff Sergeant O's torso in his arms and threw it up and over into the back of their HMMWV, like it was a bale of hay. His torso was charred, with no head, arms, or legs. Staff Sergeant K and I both turned around very quickly. "What the fuck!"

"I wish I hadn't seen that shit," K said to me.

"No fucking shit," I responded.

One of the medics walked up to me. "Sergeant Augi, can you give us a few guys to help look for other remains, please?"

"You got it, buddy," I replied. I got on my radio. "All Blue elements, listen up. I need one guy per squad to come to my location, over." They all responded and sent their soldiers over to me. I also got my medic, forward observer, and my RTO (radio operator) as well. Once they were all around me, I gave them the order they didn't quite want to hear. "All right, listen up. Put your tac lights on and begin searching the area in pairs. We got other parts of Staff Sergeant O to look for."

"Ah, man," one of the soldiers replied to me.

"Hey, I know it sucks, but let's get this shit over with so we can get the fuck out of here, you hear me?"

"Roger, Sergeant," they replied.

"Okay, move out, and let's get this shit done."

I told K that I had just eaten dinner with him last night and that he was the new EOD NCOIC. He was young, too. As I lit up another cigarette, I thought, *Now he's lying in pieces in the back of that vehicle over there.* Other shit kept running through my head as well, such as whether or not we're going to find out who the fuck did this and go after his sorry ass. I was willing to bet the answer was definitely yes.

As I was standing there thinking about all this shit, one of my soldiers walked up to me. He was trying to hand me something. "Here you go, Sergeant Augi." As I looked down at what he had in his hand, I almost shit my pants. It was a piece of Staff Sergeant O's jawbone.

"Oh shit, what the fuck? Son—get that fucking shit out of my face." After I took a deep breath, I realized I didn't give clear enough instructions on what to do with his body parts after they found them. "Go over there and give it to the medics, son," I told him.

"Roger, Sergeant."

After about half an hour of searching, I told them to go back to their squad leaders and follow their instructions. I walked over to the medics and told them that we were done searching, and they concurred. After a couple of minutes, they were done packing up the rest of his remains and with the two MP vehicles took off and headed back to FOB Saint Michael. I called in to the battalion to inform them of their departure, and they instructed me to stand by and await the Mumuhdyah Fire Department, which was bringing out a fire truck to spray off the road.

It seemed like it took forever, but eventually, the fire department showed up on the site and sprayed off the road on all four lanes. Once they were complete, I called back to headquarters again and gave them the update on the situation on the site. We were finally given the change of mission and were ordered to return to base. Thank Christ. At approximately 2300, I gave another safety/convoy briefing to my platoon, then we loaded up the vehicles and finally headed back to Saint Michael. Our assholes were puckered pretty tight on the way back. We were still about ten miles away from base and safety. After what we had just witnessed, we were all on edge on that ride back, and for the next few times outside the wire, as well. Don't get me wrong, we always maintained a high status of alertness, but that night, understandably, was a little scarier.

When we got back to the FOB, we locked and cleared our weapons and drove straight to the fuel point to fill up all our vehicles. When we got there, I got out and walked straight to the battalion operations shop (S-3). I signed my patrol back in with the time. As I did, I realized what was to be a ten- or twelve-hour day, and routine, ended up being an eighteen-hour day and sickening, with the loss of one of our soldiers. After I left battalion headquarters, I walked over to my company and briefed our commander on the day's events.

We got back to our tents, unloaded the trucks, and nobody said shit to each other. There was no episode or two of *24*. Instead, there was a night of depression and silence. I walked over to the shower trailers, took a shower, shaved, and when I got back to the tent, I told the guys to turn off the lights and go to sleep. That night, to this day sixteen years later, is the last thing I think about when I go to bed and the first thing I think about when I wake up. Every so often, I dream about it in between. My nightmare often finishes with a kid handing me half a jawbone and saying, "Here you go, Sergeant Augi . . ."

The next day around 1600, our battalion conducted his memorial service outside of the battalion headquarters. Sometimes combat is a motherfucker. One night you're having dinner with somebody you just met, and the next night, you're picking up pieces of his body that were blown up across an entire highway—fact. In April 2004, our battalion redeployed back to Fort Bragg, after we were relieved, and handed off our sectors to a Marine Corps battalion.

When I was a kid in high school, I wanted to be war veteran. I especially wished I could have gone back in time a couple of decades and be a Vietnam War veteran. After my first tour in Iraq, I said to myself, "Be careful what you wish for."

Let me make this clear, we were not victims of this war—we were on the offensive. We were not afraid of these people or their bullshit cowardly tactics. Our mission was to simply capture or kill them, period. That's exactly what we did quite often, without any regrets. I know that I am explaining reasons for me being diagnosed with PTSD, but like I said in the introduction of this book, I am and will never be a victim of it or ever feel sorry for myself. Combat is a motherfucker sometimes, right? I have seen a handful of veterans that play the system and want people to believe they are victims of their bad experiences in combat. What fucking experiences in combat aren't bad? Give me a break. I could probably end this book now with this chapter and make it a short story of my one story that continues to affect me to this day from my time in combat. Trust me, there are plenty of other stories, but I'm not going to tell you every story of every combat patrol that I went on in my three combat deployments to the Middle East. Fuck it! I won't end it; I have plenty of more shit to tell you . . .

CHAPTER 2

SEPTEMBER 2005
NEW ORLEANS, LOUISIANA

During the Iraq War, dead bodies were clearly a common thing to see but were picked up by proper authorities in a timely manner. Their corpses were respectfully gathered and either turned in to the proper authorities and/or turned over to their families, in most cases. American and Coalition Forces missions in combat were managed swiftly, as emphasized in detail in my first chapter. However, in the continental United States of America, during the aftermath of Hurricane Katrina, they were not. Instead, dead bodies remained rotting in the streets, in public parking garages, in back alleys, and in their homes. My nightmares from this period do not only derive from seeing these rotting bodies on a daily basis, but I believe primarily because of the idea that this was happing on the streets of our own country. It sickened me, as I'm sure it sickened all who were involved in this assignment from the 82nd Airborne Division and the emergency responders who were there.

My company, Headquarters Company, would be in charge of the squadron convoy that would take all vehicles down to New Orleans, led by Captain J, my company commander that I talked about in *Division*. The First Sergeant would stay back and was in charge of getting the rest of the company personnel down there with the squadron. We were to make it down there with the convoy in around the same time that the rest of the Brigade Task Force would make it down via C-17s. About nine hours after our alert and initial briefing from the Squadron Commander, me and Captain J left with the squadron convoy and started making our way down to Louisiana. On or around September 10, 2005, approximately twelve days after Hurricane Katrina hit, Task Force Panther deployed to New Orleans in support of Operation Helping Hand. This would be my last major event with the 82nd Airborne Division and definitely one that I will never forget.

It took us just under two days to get down there with the convoy. We had minimal trouble with our vehicles making the trip. I believe only one vehicle became dead-lined out of all thirty-five or forty. Overall, the mission of getting the squadron's vehicles down to New Orleans was a success. It had just turned dark when we hit the outskirts of the city. Our destination was to get to the Naval Reserve and Recruitment Center, just about a mile or so north of the French Quarter.

As we came over the Mississippi River on the Crescent City Connection Bridge, everything was blacked out. There were no lights on anywhere in the city. The only illumination was the little bit of moonlight we had. As we came over the bridge and could finally make out the skyline of the city, an eerie feeling came over me. It immediately reminded me of the movie *Escape from New York*, when Kurt Russell flew into Manhattan and the entire New York City skyline was blacked out. It seriously looked identical.

When we got into the city, the only lighting came from our headlights on the vehicles and the lights from emergency workers that had their generators on. We had received directions from one of the workers on the street on exactly how to get to the Naval Center, so we headed in that direction. It wasn't that hard to find. It was basically down a boulevard until it dead-ended and off to the right. There were signs for it as well. Once we arrived, all the vehicles remained in the parking lot, and the drivers, along with other soldiers who made the trip, just stayed in them for the remainder of the night. I want to say the Commander, Command Sergeant Major, and the staff were already at the complex waiting on us to arrive. Our First Sergeant came out and met Captain J and took us inside, where they had established our squadron headquarters.

The next morning when the sun came up, we all linked up with our soldiers that arrived the day prior. We were quartered in the offices on the first, second, and third floors. It was basically finding a space on the floor next to a desk, placing your ruck and equipment down, including our weapons, and that was our new home for the next month. There was no electricity anywhere in the city. The entire complex was completely abandoned except for our squadron that had just moved in less than twenty-four hours ago. The stench of the building we were in reeked to high Heaven of rotted meat. The meat cooler for the mess hall was rotting for the past two weeks in the heat. There was a crew cleaning and sanitizing it out as we were moving in. I'm not quite sure who they belonged to, but I wouldn't want that job for a million dollars. It was at least ninety to one hundred degrees when we got down there. Air conditioning was obviously non-existent as well.

The rest of the brigade was across the river in an old National Guard facility staying in tents. Once the entire unit was on the ground, there was no time to waste. We immediately began conducting rescue operations with other entities down there with boats. Captain J, the First Sergeant, and I rode around at first and started going down to explore some of the nearby neighborhoods. Most of the streets off the main boulevard that connected to the facility we were staying at were still underwater with no vehicle access, only accessible by boat. We made our way downtown and began making connections with FEMA representatives to see how we could help them or if they could assist us.

Later on that first day, the First Sergeant found a HMMWV on the facility that was painted blue. He actually signed for it from a representative on the compound. That blue HMMWV became our primary means of transportation for the remainder of our time in New Orleans. Every day, we drove around and checked on all areas that our soldiers were being utilized for that day. We made sure they were being taken care of with food, water, batteries for their radios, etc.

The majority of the 82nd soldiers reported to the FEMA rescue teams that were deployed throughout the city. Each day, they would cover a certain amount of areas marked off on their maps. They cleared house by house and street by street by watercraft. A company each day from 2 Panther was tasked to patrol dismounted through the French Quarter and the Bourbon Street area in order to maintain a show of presence for the prevention of criminal activity, such as looting, that had become one of the biggest crime activities since the hurricane hit two weeks prior. The water around the downtown area had begun receding, but very slowly. Around Bourbon Street, it was still ankle or even knee deep in some parts. All the northern portions of the city, where the levies had broken from Lake Pontchartrain, were completely underwater. This was where the primary rescue operations were taking place.

As we were driving through the 9th Ward District as far as our blue HMMWV would take us without getting too submerged in the water, we came across our first dead body. There was a corpse laying on top of the roof of a car with his arms slung out over the windshield. At this point, the water was up to the bottom of the windshield, just over the hood of the car. We took note of his location, turned around, and headed back towards our facility, but through a different direction. We drove along a wall that ran alongside the river heading north to where we were staying. We stopped and found our second body. This body was wrapped up in a white sheet and placed next to the wall. Above the body was a spray-painted message on the wall that said, "Fuck You Katrina," with an arrow pointing down at the body. I'll admit it; I was a little creeped out by this, especially being so close to where we were staying.

As the sun went down that first night, everything got quiet, and all you could hear were dogs in the distance that had been abandoned. Knowing the bodies were outside our compound, with the dark silence in the city, it felt like a fucking zombie movie, I'm not shitting you. Good luck trying to sleep at night with that horrid smell and the relentless heat. If you did happen to fall asleep, good luck having pleasant dreams in this environment, but we hadn't even seen the worst of it yet.

One of our companies was responsible for patrolling around and maintaining a presence at the convention center. This was a primary point of pick up where buses took the displaced citizens out of the ravaged city. There was a walkway that connected from the rear of the center to the Superdome, where thousands were seeking refuge during and after the hurricane. The mess outside the convention center was unexplainable. Diapers, MRE trash, shopping carts, clothing, you name it. Trash was piled up outside and scattered all over the place. The state had just evacuated these people a day prior to our arrival.

I remember thinking to myself, *How is this ever going to get cleaned up to where people can come here again without chance of disease?* It was disgusting. First Sergeant, Captain J, and I thought we had seen the worst until we decided to walk over to the Superdome. From the point we entered into the stadium from the walkway of the convention center, we had come out into the parking garage on the second or third floor. The first floor was underwater. It was real dark inside, so I turned on the tac-light on my M-4 for lighting. The smell was terrible. The floor underneath us was flooded, and all you could see were the roofs of the vehicles. "Oh shit!" I shouted out. There was a body floating face down in the parking lot underneath us. His face was peeled back on both sides of his head from laying and rotting in the water for obviously quite a while by this time, we estimated from the hurricane itself two weeks ago. I shined my light further down. He had a perfect water bottle in the back pocket of his jeans. "Oh, look, a water bottle."

"He couldn't keep his face on, but that damn water bottle is in perfect condition," one of us said—I can't quite remember who. "That's the water boy, Bobby Boucher." We shook our heads, and the name stuck with us.

When we entered the dome itself, it was the same scene that was at the convention center. Diapers piled up and trash everywhere. I'm sure there were some dead bodies in there, too, but we didn't stick around too long because it was so hot. We looked down on the football field, which was covered in water, and it had trash floating on top of it as well. I remember thinking the city of New Orleans was going to have to tear this place down and rebuild it for sanitation reasons, if they ever wanted people to come back to this place.

When we got back to the convention center, I told a FEMA guy about "Bobby Boucher" floating in the parking garage of the Superdome. Captain J also told them about the other two bodies that were over by the Naval Complex, too. He told us that the team they had with them couldn't do anything about the bodies, that it wasn't their jurisdiction, that it was for a different FEMA team that had not made it to the city yet. It made no sense to any of us. As a matter of fact, nothing about this disaster relief was making sense, ever since it had begun two weeks before.

We asked the First Sergeant there at the center if his soldiers needed anything from us that we could bring back for them. He said he needed more batteries for his radios. "We'll be back with some for you, First Sergeant, no problem," I told him. When we left in the blue HMMWV, I had to ask, "Do either of you find it completely fucked up that there are bodies still laying out in this city two weeks later?"

The First Sergeant said, "Yeah, because the correct department for body disposal isn't here yet . . ." We were actually not only sickened by this thought but couldn't believe the reactions of these FEMA representatives.

The next day or so, we traveled north as far as we could on I-10 to check out a boat launch area that FEMA had designated as a launch and recovery point. They were launching the boats from an exit ramp off the interstate. As we were driving to the site, we drove past another body. This one was wrapped in black trash bags. The body had bloated so much that it was popping through the bag and had one arm hanging out. On the side of a U.S. interstate, no shit, can't make this up. Captain J said, "That's Chester."

I said, "What the fuck?"

"Yeah, that's 'Chester, Chester, the I-10 Infester.'"

Me and the First Sergeant looked at him and said, "Okay, that's his name." It's how we were making ourselves deal with what we were seeing in the streets of the United States. Hell, bodies in Iraq didn't stay out in the open this long—only in America . . .

The more we went out into the neighborhoods, the more paranoid I was getting. Not about people coming after us or anything, but the dogs that were becoming violent. They had been swimming in this shit for weeks now, starving, eating God knew what or who, and I could only imagine. We would be driving through one of these neighborhoods, and all of a sudden, a dog would jump out, barking and acting all crazy. I started locking and loading my M-4, which we weren't supposed to do, but like I told Captain J and the First Sergeant, "I'll be damned if I'm going to get bit by one of these pitbulls or rottweilers." Neither one of them said shit to me. Our blue HMMWV didn't have doors on it, so I could see one of those wild, ravaged bastards trying to jump in our vehicle like Cujo or some shit.

We would sit outside at night at the Naval Center and shoot the shit about some of the bullshit we would see that day. Some crazy stuff would come out of our mouths, too.

"So, we have 'Bobby Boucher' and 'Chester, Chester, the I-10 Infester,'" the First Sergeant said.

"Yeah, but what about the guy that's on top of the car a block down the street?"

Captain J suggested that we refer to him as "Blue."

I asked, "Why Blue? What's the significance of the name Blue?"

"I don't know," he replied, "from the movie *Old School*. You're my boy Blue!" Captain J paused a moment then said, "Okay, his name is Blue from here on out. Are we three in agreement? Because we can't fuck this up."

"Oh yeah, Blue it is." We never did name the body that was behind the complex, against the wall.

I went upstairs through the dark-ass stairwell, waiting for a zombie or some shit to jump out at me. The smell of the rotten meat was dissipating. I made it to my rucksack, pulled out my wooby (poncho liner), went back downstairs to the open outdoors, put a cot together, and slept outside. I tried to fall asleep, but it took a while with the dogs barking in the distance. I kept my weapon snuggled up to me as I laid on my cot, trying to fall asleep, and after a little while, I eventually did.

I was woken up a couple of hours later. "Sergeant. Hey, Sergeant."

I rolled over. "Yeah, what's up? What do you need?"

"I found this in the parking lot and figured you wanted it." It was the soldier handing me the piece of jawbone from Iraq. I woke up hollering and immediately sat up on the cot. I could hear the dogs still barking in the nearby distance outside of our perimeter. It was creepy. I reached under my cot and grabbed my pack of cigarettes and lit one up. As I smoked it, I put both hands on my forehead and put my head down. Up to this point, this wasn't the first time I had this guy in my dreams. Seventeen years later, he still comes to visit me with the jawbone in his hand . . .

CHAPTER 3

OCTOBER 2000
DRILL SERGEANT SCHOOL

Before I begin talking to you about my experiences in Army Drill Sergeant School, I have to tell you a story that I still dream about from time to time. It was about a year before I got levied for drill sergeant duty, and we were conducting a training exercise at Fort Bragg. We were in the field. Just a few days prior, there had been a serious accident with a soldier that was assigned to our battalion. I didn't know him well, but I believe he was in Headquarters Company. I remember seeing him around the battalion mess hall and formations. He was a young sergeant who was in the middle of Jumpmaster School. During the practical exercise of the aircraft portion in the school, he was killed.

During his testing on putting jumpers out of the aircraft, he went to do his initial or final clear to the rear; I'm not sure which. This means that the Jumpmaster leans out of the door of the aircraft and inspects to ensure there is nothing there that could hinder the soldier's safety while jumping, such as ripped metal on the aircraft itself. When he pulled himself back inside the aircraft, his rip cord grip from his reserve parachute got caught on the side of the door. It immediately deployed his reserve parachute, pulling his body outside the aircraft, feet first. When his main parachute opened, his body was practically upside down. The risers from his main parachute ripped off his head.

This gruesome fact was discovered upon the investigation and after the drop zone recovery team found his body in the trees, a few hundred meters from the edge of the drop zone. When they got to him, his lifeless body was suspended in the trees because his parachute got caught up in the thick-wooded area. It was only when they pulled him out of the tree that he was hanging from that they discovered he was decapitated. The sergeant in charge of the detail told the team that they had to look for his head.

About a week later, our platoon was in the field in the exact area that they had found this man's body. I remember how creepy it was because we actually had to sleep on the ground in that area. One of my fellow squad leaders had said that it was almost the same location that they found him. I remember the night we stayed out there, I had a nightmare of him walking out of the woods and up to me. He asked me, "Hey, Sergeant Augi, did you happen to find my head tonight?" I sat up in the dark and lit up a cigarette. I was so creeped out that I couldn't get back to sleep. All I wanted was to just simply move the platoon out of the area, which we did at first light.

I told this story in this chapter because it seemed too short to make it its own chapter, and it carries relevance to the subject of this book. I figured the best place for it was at the beginning of my drill sergeant time, since it made an appearance in my thoughts often during this portion of my time in the Army. I guess the horror of the situation was still fresh in my mind. This accident took place approximately a year before I left for drill sergeant duty.

In the U.S. Army, drill sergeant duty is a two-year additional assignment for young noncommissioned officers (NCOs), where they train brand new recruits into becoming soldiers. During this time, the drill sergeants are given nine weeks to teach, coach, and mentor young civilians into becoming highly trained, disciplined, and proficient soldiers. A Basic Combat Training Drill Sergeant will endure approximately between ten to twelve Basic Training cycles during their two years. The timeline begins when the Drill Sergeant gets assigned and reports to their basic training company and ends exactly two years later to that exact month upon which they reported. This is known throughout the Army as "the Trail."

You, the reader may ask, "What does being a drill sergeant have to do with PTSD?" Well, for me, I still have bad dreams of screaming and hollering at soldiers. My wife still wakes me up to this day because I begin yelling and cursing in my sleep. She will elaborate more in detail when you get to her excerpt later on. Also, like Drill Sergeant School, or any other military school I've been to, I have a fear of failing. Therefore, I still to this day have dreams of going through these schools and failing in the dream. When I eventually wake up, primarily when my wife has to wake me up, I'm in a cold sweat. It usually takes me a second to get back into reality and remember where I am at. When I do, I calm down and realize I already passed that school, and it was in the past—that I am retired and out of the Army now. I might have already said this once during this book, but my biggest fear in my twenty years of service in the military was not combat, jumping out of airplanes, or live-fire maneuver ranges. It was failure at a task I was responsible for or a school I had to graduate from for career progression.

The year was 2000, and Basic Combat Training (BCT) was the initial nine weeks that every soldier endured in the Army. Jobs in the Army are also known as Military Occupational Skills (MOSs), and most combat arms MOSs in the Army had their own BCTs. These training cycles were extended for twelve to thirteen weeks, which included an additional month of their specific job training. These MOSs usually consisted of Infantry, Artillery, and Engineers and, at the time, were all male only. Any other BCT programs were designed to be coed, with separate barracks for male and female recruits. Each platoon consisted of approximately three drill sergeants—two male and one female—and one of them usually were a combat arms MOS. The average was three drill sergeants to approximately sixty to seventy recruits.

Fort Jackson, South Carolina, was the premier BCT Army Training Installation in those days and probably still is today. The coed environment was still a relatively newer concept that was introduced around the mid-nineties throughout the Army. Some leaders during this time period still had issues with this concept, for more reasons than one. It wasn't about physical stamina, training standards, or even the different appearances of the recruits. It was the reality of having both male and female eighteen-year-olds spending twenty-four hours a day with each other for a nine-week cycle. This added more stress to an already stressful environment. The term "fraternization" became as common in the BCT environment as the term "training" itself.

I may repeat this periodically throughout the next couple of chapters. The success of a good drill sergeant is not how much you can scream and holler at someone. The success of a good drill sergeant is being able to teach—period. For two years on the Trail, I witnessed drill sergeants fail with their jobs because they could not connect with the recruits. All they could do was scream all the time at them, day in and day out. As time went on, and not too much time, either, the recruits simply would lose all respect for that particular drill sergeant that just screamed at them all the time. A recruit, or any other subordinate soldier back in a regular unit, will respect a leader that can teach them something instead of yelling at them consistently. I am not at all suggesting being soft on them, and I was not, but there definitely is a time for teaching and raising your voice.

After one BCT cycle went by, I realized that the recruits were giving themselves a sense of pride in learning something, especially when it came to learning soldier skills. A successful drill sergeant must also realize that these young eighteen- and nineteen-year-olds volunteered to be part of this environment and that they were not drafted as some of our fathers were. They actually wanted and craved to be there in order to be a part of a premier military force. I also was not afraid to tell them, "Good job," when they completed a task that they learned to do to standard. By doing this, I and many other drill sergeants had earned their respect, which goes a long way in that environment. I still remember what my boss, the Senior Drill of our platoon, told me when I first got on the Trail. He said to me, "Your success for the next two years isn't what you accomplish anymore but what your soldiers accomplish." Now that I have the drill sergeant concept down, I'll explain how it begins in Drill Sergeant School.

"First and Second Squad, FALL OUT, U-Formation, FALL IN. RELAX. LET ME HAVE YOUR ATTENTION. The next position, which I will name, explain, have demonstrated, and which you will conduct practical work on, is the position of attention. The position of attention is the key position for all stationary, facing, and marching movements. The commands for this position are FALL IN and ATTENTION."

This was going to be my reality for the next two years of my life and in even more detail for the next nine weeks during this school. I never wanted to or expected to ever become a drill sergeant. As a matter of fact, I'm quite sure that eighty percent of drills sergeants and/or former "drills" never expected or wanted to, either. Just like most Army recruiters do not wish to be or have not asked to become recruiters. Drill sergeant and recruiting duty in the Army are additional duties that about fifty percent of sergeants, staff sergeants, and a few sergeants first class get levied for throughout their military careers. "Levied" is a nice military term for being drafted to a duty station or an additional duty. As an infantryman stationed at Fort Bragg, North Carolina, in the summer of 2000, I too got my levy notice in the mail to attend the United States Army Drill Sergeant School or USADSS at Fort Jackson, South Carolina. Within the same notice, I was informed that my two-year drill sergeant (DS) duty was to be fulfilled at Fort Jackson after graduation as well.

Like I opened up with, I wasn't a big fan, especially coming from a combat arms MOS and going to a coed basic training environment. Many of us NCOs throughout the Army had already heard of the horror stories of male drill sergeants getting into trouble with the female recruits. There were many rumors, supported by factual incidences throughout the Army during this time, that some drill sergeants were being charged, and even went to prison for, abusing and having sexual affairs with new soldiers they were in charge of during basic training. It even got to the point that many NCOs would say that if they were ever to be levied for drill duty, they would demand and fight to get stationed at Fort Benning or another basic training installation where it was strictly combat arms so that they would be surrounded by all male soldiers instead.

I remember thinking that all it would take is to be disciplined, do the right thing, and you would have nothing to worry about. However, the Army was starting to go through a time of "political correctness," and adding a coed basic training to it could simply add fuel to the fire. Something else to think about when knowing you were going to this environment for two years as a drill sergeant is that you may be doing the right thing at all times, but what if the female recruit claims different? Could you find yourself in a guilty until proven innocent situation? One fact about being a drill sergeant in the Army, and after talking to some other drills from the other branches of service, it either makes or breaks your career. I have known some individuals that it broke their career. These were some of the thoughts that ran through my mind as I was mentally preparing for this upcoming change of life and duty assignment.

Like everything else in the Army, I treated it as a "one step at a time" scenario. Before I had to worry about being a drill sergeant, I first needed to worry about getting through Drill Sergeant School itself. Everybody knew that this was not an easy task by itself, either. One has to modulate almost all drill and ceremony steps and procedures in order to graduate. Modulating is reciting word for word each sentence and page of a marching movement, straight out of the Army Field Manual or Regulation. I remember when I was at the Basic Noncommissioned Officer's Academy (BNCOC) at Fort Benning, a couple of years prior, there were guys walking around behind the barracks we stayed at, and they were talking to themselves. The USADSS at Fort Benning was behind our company. Come to find out, they were DSS candidates that were practicing their modulating on drill and ceremony movements. They would be out there all hours of the night, too. I would walk down to the latrine at midnight to take a piss and would hear a guy talking to himself. I'd look outside the window, and bigger than shit, he'd be smoking a cigarette, pacing back and forth, modulating to himself. You have to modulate to graduate. During this timeline, the Army had three Drill Sergeant Schools, one at Fort Leonard Wood, Missouri; one at Fort Benning, Georgia; and another at Fort Jackson, South Carolina. Today, there is only one at Fort Jackson, and it is called the United States Army Drill Sergeant Academy.

I remember there were two of us within my battalion at Fort Bragg that were heading off to DSS, but to two different locations. The other NCO was heading off to Fort Benning, and I was heading to Jackson. The Battalion School's NCO advised us to pre-learn the first three modules and the Drill Sergeant Creed prior to reporting to school. We were confused and had to ask if we were going to get tested on the modules during the first week. He told us no, but it would make our lives easier for that first week's transition if we already had them memorized, the logic being that, during the transition of going back into the basic training mentality ourselves, with drill sergeants over us, knowing these modules would be one less thing to worry about and study for. So I learned the first three, which were the Position of Attention, Rest Positions at the Halt, the Hand Salute, and the Drill Sergeant's Creed, which was a couple of paragraphs by itself.

The Battalion Command Sergeant Major (CSM) also came out to give us a last-minute word of advice. He reminded us that we were heading to an NCO academy and to not take it likely. NCO academies have an academic evaluation form attached to them upon your graduation, which does get filed in your official Army records. The academic evaluation is called a DA Form 1059, and throughout school, it was pretty much thrown in our faces for the entire nine weeks that we needed it to be successful. Receive a substandard 1059 from any military leadership academy and it could be the difference of not being selected for the next promotion. Even though I was not excited about becoming a drill sergeant initially, when I received my levy notice, I still had every intention of giving one hundred ten percent at the school and afterwards giving the same effort as a drill itself for the next two years.

Fort Jackson was only about a two-and-a-half-hour drive from Fort Bragg, so the trip down there was easy. The most difficult part was finding the school itself once I arrived on post. These were the days before smartphones and the GPS systems that everyone uses today, so I had to use signs to get there. DSS on Fort Jackson is on the backside of the installation, away from the main post, so it took some searching before I finally found it.

As I entered the building, there was a Drill Sergeant Instructor (DSI) sitting at a desk as soon as I walked in. As I stood in front of him, I noticed he was the same rank as I was, a staff sergeant. He asked me if I was reporting into DSS. I replied with, "Yes, I am." He looked at me with a strange look in his eye. Before he even said anything back to me, I knew what was going to come out of his mouth next.

"Yes, I am, Drill Sergeant," he said to me with a confident tone in his voice.

I repeated, "Yes, I am, Drill Sergeant," as I half-ass slid into the position of Parade Rest. He handed me a form to fill out and asked if I drove my own privately owned vehicle. "Yes, I do, Drill Sergeant." He then instructed me to go get all my gear from my vehicle and then lock it up because it would be the last time that I would have access to the parking lot for the next three weeks. He then called for another DS candidate, who walked out of an office down the hallway. He instructed him to take me upstairs and to get me squared away.

"Sergeant, he'll take you upstairs and show you your room, bunk, and wall locker. Take all your gear up to your room. Do not unpack. Do not make your bunk. Get into PT uniform and be standing out front here for an 1800 formation, where we will conduct an introduction to the school, followed by a weigh-in."

"Yes, Drill Sergeant," I replied. I assumed not unpacking our gear was protocol in the event that someone showed up overweight. That way, they weren't wasting time setting up their area in the barracks. They could simply pick up their negative DA 1059 and drive their butts back to their duty station. It made sense to me.

Formation was not what I expected. I was guessing, prior to, that it was going to consist of a lot of yelling and in your face shit from the DSIs. It wasn't any of that. Instead, it was very professional, with all the DSIs lined up at Parade Rest with the Company Senior Drill Sergeant out front. All of us candidates were already assigned to platoons and squads and, prior to the formation, were instructed to move into our correct spots. Actually, for the first initial formation of about one hundred twenty candidates, I was impressed on how well organized this group of cadre were executing it. I could tell this was not your usual NCO academy where the cadre seem to come out lackadaisical at first until the groups get themselves organized. These were professionals that knew their jobs inside and out, and after completing two years on the Trail, one could understand how simple it was for them to be subject matter experts at this environment. These were the cream of the crop drill sergeants that had already completed two years of successful time as BCT Drills. Most of them were volunteers for a third year to be conducted at the School House on Fort Jackson. Like I said, though, they had to complete their two years down where the rubber meets the road, in the hostile chaos of the basic training environment, and do it without a blemish on their record, in order to get into the School House.

The Senior Drill Sergeant started the formation by citing the Drill Sergeant Creed to us all. After he was finished, he began giving the introduction to us. "Welcome to the United States Army Drill Sergeant School. Congratulations, you all have been selected as the top ten percent of Noncommissioned Officers' Corps, and we are in charge!" This was basically the speech that he gave the company before turning our platoons over to our DSIs. They got us back into the barracks and began the weigh-ins. I believe one DS candidate did not meet Army height and weight standard, and he or she was immediately removed from the school and sent home. There's always one.

After the weigh-in, we were sent upstairs to unpack and get our bunks and wall lockers squared away. It was back to the basic training wall locker and bunk display that every soldier, airman, sailor, and marine hated. During this time, they even had us bundle up our civilian clothes that we wore down there and turn them in downstairs. Just like brand new recruits, each DS candidate was allowed to bring one personal gym bag to store all of our civilian clothes and even our vehicle keys in. They were not kidding. You were not going to get access to that parking lot for the entire Red Phase of training, which was the first three weeks. With each passing moment that first night, reality was setting in that we were going back to basic training. The only difference this time was that they called you "Sergeant" instead of "Private." Back when I went to basic training, ten years prior, they called you some more colorful names such as "shithead," "shit for brains," "dumbass," etc.

Day one of DSS began at around 0530 with a room, wall locker, and bunk inspection by the DSIs. I had my shit squared away and stayed up pretty much most of the night getting it done. As I did my wall locker, the memories were all coming back, especially when I had to start canoe rolling my socks. Each hanger had three fingers space in between them with our unit insignia or patch on our BDUs facing towards us. Some others in my room chose to blow off getting their area set up and perhaps get to it some other time.

When the DSIs came into our room of six candidates, not one of us had our displays to their standard, which we pretty much predicted.

I figured as much. The one or two NCOs in our room that chose to do nothing all night really drew in the attention of the drills for simply not complying with their instructions to have it all completed by first call. We even had to have our last names and last four of our social security number stenciled on a piece of masking tape on the foot of our bunks and on the upper right-hand corner of our wall locker. "Hey, Sarnt, why did you choose to not comply with our instructions to have your displays finished by first call this morning?" We quickly learned that "Sergeant" turned into the one-syllable word "Sarnt" by the DSIs.

"I fell asleep," my roommate responded.

I thought to myself, *Damn, he didn't even call him "Sergeant" or "Drill Sergeant," for Christ's sake.*

"You fell asleep what?"

"I fell asleep, Drill Sergeant." The DSI did something at that point that made me and everyone else in the room realize what their strategy to earn our obedience and compliance with their instructions was going to be from here on out. They were going to take our time from us, and time in DSS is precious.

"Okay, Sarnt, after the APFT and chow this morning, you will be setting up your wall locker and bunk displays to standard. At 0900, we will begin our first demonstrated class on the first three modules that you will be tested on next week. Instead of receiving our much-needed demonstration, you will be in here setting up your area." That was it. The DSIs walked out of the room and went into the next, and we went down to formation in our PT uniforms and with one canteen of water. There was no screaming or making anybody do push-ups or any of that, simply taking time away on a critical event such as our first module demonstration. That's how they knew they had us. Fail any written or verbal exam in this leadership academy, you will fail the school, and your military career will probably end. It was that simple.

The 0600 formation started off with the Senior Drill Sergeant calling out one candidate to come out front and begin the Drill

Sergeant Creed in front of the company. As he or she said each line of the creed, the rest of the company had to repeat it loudly and thunderously. This would occur every morning for the next nine weeks. Everybody was going to get an opportunity to be out front, so it behooved everyone to learn the damn thing.

The Army Physical Fitness Test, or the APFT, or as we referred to it most of the time, the PT Test, was the first evaluation event of day one. They marched us down the hill to a large outdoor arena area with a track. We began stretching and counting off the seconds of each stretch to their standards. Each event was graded to Army standard. If the candidate failed any event of the PT Test, they were given one opportunity to conduct one retest. If they failed it twice, they were removed from the course as a PT failure. Try going back to your unit and explain that one to your first sergeant or command sergeant major. The standard of first passing an APFT before continuing on in a course was not limited to DSS but was the normal procedure for all other NCO academies throughout the Army. Nevertheless, we lost another two or three candidates for being PT failures that first week.

We were moving fast that first day, and there was no slowing down. Like the DSI said in our room earlier, at 0900, we received our first demonstrations on the Position of Attention, Rest Positions at the Halt, and the Hand Salute. All three modules would be tested on week two. Being tested on all three modules that were presented at the beginning of the school week only happened once throughout the school. These three modules in particular every DS candidate had to say, verbatim, in order to pass. After that, the number of modules increased depending on the drill and ceremony subject. For example, the subjects consisted of Facing Movements at the Halt, Steps and Marching, Basic Manual of Arms, Advanced Manual of Arms, and Squad and Platoon Drill. Each subject had between three to eight drills we had to learn within them.

DSIs would demonstrate all the modules of that particular subject for that week to learn and study, but we would only have to pitch one or maybe two of them. We just didn't know which one it would be, so you couldn't blow any of them off. You had to learn all of them verbatim. When it became test time, it would be one-on-one with you and one DSI that would grade you. You normally would be allowed to have one demonstrator, which was another candidate. If you were doing a marching module, you could have several individuals demonstrate for you while you pitched the module to the DSI. The DSI picked which movements you would modulate by having the candidate to be tested roll a die. Whatever number your die landed on was the module you got tested on. If you had to do two modules within that subject, you would simply roll the die again.

It definitely was a fair concept, but I'll be damned if I always rolled the hardest module for that particular week. I mean every time. It was a good thing that I had already memorized all three for this week, because it did make that initial change of environment easier. The DSIs warned us not to get ahead and try to learn more than what we were presented for each week. The logic was that you did not want to overload yourself. Module testing was not the only testing we had for any given week, either. There would be written exams, and any other events that all candidates had to pass in order to graduate, such as weapons qualification, and every other basic training graduation requirement that a new recruit had to do.

We were in Red Phase, which meant total lockdown. No phones, no vehicles, only written letters, and no leaving the school area. We had the red guide-on (flag) in front of each platoon. Our structure was the exact same as that of a basic training company. Each platoon had a Platoon Guide out front. Next to him or her was the Guide-on Bearer. Each platoon was broken down into four squads with assigned squad leaders for each. Some of us candidates were still in shock that we were having to transition all we knew into a basic training mentality. Some of us couldn't get over it, either.

During that first week of school, there was one Sergeant First Class (E-7) candidate that simply could not accept the fact that he was there and that he was on his way to being a drill sergeant for the next two years. This guy had a piss-poor attitude from the start and bitched about everything. Yeah, it sucked, and we all preferred to be somewhere else, doing something different, but we weren't and had to suck it up and drive on. This guy refused to accept being there and would tell me he had no intention of staying. I used to ask him how he planned on getting out of the school, and he would tell me that he was going to talk to the Commandant and get the hell out of here.

The commandant of any NCO academy is a command sergeant major, which is the highest enlisted rank in any branch of service, and you usually are not going to bullshit them, either. The guy trying to get out was assigned to Fort Bragg prior to school and was infantry as well. According to him, he had just begun his rifle platoon sergeant time and needed to get back to continue it. I just remember thinking, *Well, good luck thinking you're going to get out of here on a positive note. The cadre here, in this place, isn't going to give two shits about your platoon sergeant time at Fort Bragg.* My logic happened to be spot on. He had gone to our Senior Platoon DSI and complained, which ended up with the Company Senior DSI, and finally with the Commandant of the academy.

The next day, I asked him how it went with the Commandant. He told me that they all were trying to convince him to stay and that it would be beneficial for his career progression, which was absolutely true. He felt differently because he was already an E-7. I told him that it would probably guarantee him his E-8 promotion. How convenient would that be? Start off as a senior drill sergeant for a little while, make the E-8 promotion list, and move right into being a basic training first sergeant. This seemed pretty simple to me. Nope! This guy was "Ranger Rick" and wanted to get back to "Ranger Land" at Fort Bragg—no matter what it took to get there. He was pretty much an asshole with an attitude like he was beyond becoming a drill. At least that was my perception of him. I ran into a couple of those guys during my time on the Trail.

He had admitted to me what his plan for getting out of there was going to be. He intended to purposely fail the first written exam twice, so that he would be an academic failure for the course. I asked to him, "You sure you want to do that, Sergeant? You know you're going to get a bad 1059 on your record, right?"

He said back, "I don't give a shit about all that. I'm gonna get the fuck out of this place and get back to a line unit where I belong." I just shook my head in disbelief. I didn't ask or want to be there, either, but I wasn't going to end my career over it. Instead, like I said earlier, I had every intention to do my best both in the school and on the Trail.

So he failed the written exam both times, and his release procedures began immediately. When he came out of the Commandant's office, he was pissed. Apparently, the Commandant had called his Battalion Command Sergeant Major back at Fort Bragg, and he was notified that for his actions of purposely failing DSS, he would also lose his opportunity to be a platoon sergeant back there as well. When he told me this news, I wasn't surprised at all. Coming from Fort Bragg myself, I knew the politics of it, and he should have also. He said he had a connection in Ranger Branch and that he was going to go back to Ranger Training Brigade at Fort Benning, where he would finish out his career as an E-7. I told him good luck and maybe I'd be seeing him around someday. Unfortunately, that's exactly what happened. About three years down the road, he would end up being one of my Ranger Instructors, and I would regret that I had ever even met him. I talked about him, and what I had to go through since he knew that I knew about how he got out of DSS, in my second book *Roster Number Five-Zero*.

Marching into the chow hall was not an easy task anymore, either. We would march in as a platoon and file in by squads. "File from the left, column half left!" As the First Squad Leader, I looked over my right shoulder and gave the command, "Column half left!" When the DSI gave the command March, I stepped off with the wrong foot. He immediately caught me and got into my face.

"You stepped off with the wrong foot, Sarnt. RBI that and have it on my desk prior to morning formation tomorrow." Now RBI was an acronym in DSS for Response Based Indorsement. Yes, I am aware that the word Indorsement is misspelled. Or is it? Indorsement is still in the dictionary and has the same meaning as endorsement. Anyway, in Drill Sergeant School, having to RBI a drill and ceremony movement was considered punishment by us candidates. The DSIs would argue that it was a learning tool to correct one's mistakes. Both are correct. Again, either way, that shit took time away from us, time that could be used for studying a module or for an upcoming written exam. When you were told to RBI a movement you may have screwed up on during the training day, that meant on your personal time to handwrite the correct way to perform it, right out of the Drill and Ceremony Field Manual. Anyway, I RBI'd the correct foot to step off with on a column half left movement and had it on the Drill Sergeant's desk that evening.

Marching to cadence while singing was the only way of life these days during Drill Sergeant School. "One, two, three, four! DSS, DSS! One, two, three, four! DSS, DSS!" We were getting on buses and being taken over to main post, straight in the heart of basic combat training land. We were about to do Fort Jackson's Victory Tower for the next few hours. Victory Tower was a forty-foot rappel tower with other rope bridge obstacles around it as well. Each candidate is given a class in the rope corral pit on how to properly put on a rappel seat prior to walking up the steps to the top of the tower. Once on top, the drill sergeant would link the candidate into the main rope and send them over down the tower. The most difficult part was getting each student into a proper L-shape before sending them down. Later on, we found it to be the same challenge with the recruits once on the Trail.

The entire morning at Victory Tower, I was waiting for the range cadre or the DSIs to show us how to run the range itself as drill sergeants. That never happened. We would simply run through these ranges as if we were basic trainees ourselves, and that was it!

I soon figured out that learning how to run these training facilities was going to be taught by our drill sergeant buddies once we got to BCT. Most of the Range NCOs in this environment were ex-drills or NCOs that were broken. Broken is a military slang term meaning injured. Most of them pretty much acted as if their job was more important than yours. I also learned this really quick when I got on the Trail. The funny part is that any BCT drill sergeant could do their own job plus their job, too, any day of the week.

Our instructors would get us together as platoons every so often and talk to us about the realities of the Trail. "Hey, sarnts, I know this sucks for ya. It did for us, too. Who the hell wants to leave the regular Army and come into this environment? We sure as hell didn't want to, either. But let me tell you something, sarnts, being here in Drill Sergeant School is nothing compared to the world you all are about to enter in a few weeks. DSS is a frickin' cake walk, sarnts. The BCT world is insane. You'll be dealing with sixty-five eighteen-year-olds day in and day out. Getting them through the chow hall is a task by itself. They ought to allow us to give you a class on that by itself, but they won't put it in the curriculum. It's going to stink. I mean literally your barracks, being in a closed setting with all those kids, is going to smell. Some of them are not going to shower or the air conditioning is going to give out in your bays, and it's going to stink. So prepare yourselves, sarnts. Later on, in Blue Phase, you'll have an opportunity to go spend a day in BCT, as kind of a hands-on training day, so that you can see it up front for yourselves."

After the Bayonet Assault Course, the Fort Jackson Obstacle Course, and the Gas Chamber, on top of more module testing and written exams in between, we were ready to change the guide-ons to White Phase. We were put into a company formation with the traditional Basic Training Phase Change Ceremony, where the Drills would change each guide-on from red to white. This meant more to us than just knowing we were moving on to the next phase of the school, but that we were going to get a little more freedom given back to us. Like I said, this was designed to take us through almost identically what the privates go through in BCT. This weekend was going to be the first time in three weeks we could leave the academy area on our own. We were even given the opportunity to go on a pass for the whole weekend. The DSIs opened up the storage closet in the barracks and let us get our personal bags with our civilian clothes. I ended up driving back to Fort Bragg to stay with my pregnant wife for the weekend. Honestly, instead of relaxing all weekend, I ended up having her help me study for the next group of modules I had to learn for the upcoming week.

White Phase, just like BCT, was primarily focused on marksmanship training and qualification. Every soldier must qualify with an M16A2 rifle to graduate from basic training. Same rules applied to DSS candidates. The M16 was the assault rifle for that time but was still considered old for most infantry personnel because we had mostly already switched over to using the M-4 Carbine. The M-4 is a smaller, lighter version of the M16 but has the same mechanical functions.

"One, two, three, four! DSS, DSS! One, two, three, four! DSS, DSS!" We marched with our rifles at the position of Port Arms and filed onto the buses, heading to our first rifle range. Once there, we filed into the bleachers, and the DSIs began to give us our range safety briefing. This was the zero range, and for those that do not understand military marksmanship, zeroing is putting the bullets or rounds on your point of aim through your sites on the weapon. This is done by adjusting windage and elevation on the sites (up and down, left and right). The standard is placing five consecutive rounds, out of nine, inside of a four-centimeter circle on a target while in a foxhole-supported position. The target is twenty-five meters from your position.

The briefing also consisted of the DSIs telling us that if we were combat arms MOSs to not do our own thing while setting up our foxholes for firing. It was almost insulting to have someone tell us how to properly set up a supported firing position, but it was part of the standard training, and we would have to comply—just like every other aspect of the school. I remember getting into the foxhole, by command of the range tower, and placing our non-firing arms out on the dirt in front of us. We were then instructed to draw a line along our arm and then cross it where our wrist lay. That's the spot we would set up our sandbags to lay our non-firing arms. I remember thinking how ridiculous this was.

The weapons qualification portion of DSS was painful, due to having to comply with these little rules that were given to us, but at the end of the day, most of us qualified and passed another mandatory test in order to graduate. Notice I said "most of us" qualified with our rifles. Yes, there were some NCOs in the school that had problems qualifying, but if memory serves me correctly, they eventually did. The problem was we were moving along with the other required classes and testing at the school, and not qualifying meant a DSI had to take them back out to the range. The rest of us were moving on while others were getting behind, having to still worry about qualification.

The school moved on, and eventually, we entered the final three weeks and Blue Phase. The testing was getting more difficult, especially the modules. By this final phase, we were being tested on Squad and Platoon Drills. Of course, as I explained earlier, I rolled the die on the more difficult modules such as Count Off, Stack Arms, and Take Arms during Squad Drill. During Platoon Drill, I rolled Counter Column, and I believe everyone had to do Opening Ranks and Closing Ranks, according to academy standards. When a candidate was finished with their module, the DSI would sound off with, "Close it out, Sarnt." The candidate would reply with, "At normal cadence, At Ease." The term "close it out" was a way of the Trail. From DSS until my two years ended at Fort Jackson, saying "close it out" was a more respectful way of saying shut up. Forgive me if I continue to say, "I believe" or "if I remember correctly." After all, this was twenty years ago for me. Just typing that sentence alone makes me feel old.

We did have our visiting BCT for a day during Blue Phase. We got dropped off at a BCT battalion just prior to their PT formation. We were broken down into platoons and sent to the respected platoon offices or command posts (CPs). I know for a fact that the drill sergeants did not want us there and didn't need or want our help, either. I remember going through the ranks in the morning looking at the recruits and yelling at some of them for moving at the position of attention or whatever. Their actual drill sergeants just looked at me with disgust in their eyes. I immediately got their vibe and backed off. I went to the back of the formation and simply sat back for the rest of the day and observed. How do I know they did not want us there? Simple: when I was on the Trail, I too did not want those damn "schoolhouse candidates" yelling at or telling my soldiers what to do, either. I'll get into this a little later, but there comes a certain bond between a drill sergeant and their recruits. Almost like a mother figure protecting her own from outside elements. That's how it was with a drill and his or her soldiers.

They took us over to the Uniform Issue Facility, not to be mistaken for the Clothing Issue Facility, or CIF, but where the recruits got their phase two clothing issues. This consisted of their dress uniforms issue, fitting, and altering. Phase one was done while they were in the Replacement Center, and that issue consisted of their basic issue of uniforms such as their battle dress uniforms, PTs, socks and underwear, etc. Tactical gear, in those days, was issued at platoon level by their drill sergeants in BCT.

This was actually our first site where we were taught, and given a walk through, on their clothing issue procedures. After that was complete, we were taken over to the post CIF, where we were issued our first Drill Sergeant Campaign Hats. We were issued these during the end of the course because it was part of the graduation ceremony. When we got back to the academy, the DSIs took us to our platoon classrooms and gave us a block of instruction on how to put them together with the leather strap, how to properly fit it to our heads, and finally, how to wear the damn things.

We took the final PT Test, which prevented me from getting Distinguished Honor Graduate by a couple of points. The Honor Grad got a perfect three hundred on the test, and I got like a two hundred ninety–something. However, I did make the Commandant's List, and that was okay with me, since I had never done that good at any other leadership academy prior to. Hell, the Basic Noncommissioned Officer Academy was a two-month party for most of us, upon which I was simply lucky I graduated from, now that I look back to my mid-twenties.

With that in mind, prior to the end of the course, we were allowed to leave post overnight if we wanted to. It was like an overnight pass like the recruits get in basic training prior to their graduation. I decided to stay in the barracks and not test Murphy's Law. In other words, I didn't want to risk anything that was going to cause me to be late or get me into trouble, period. Every class always has one. One candidate ended up getting a drunk driving charge and was immediately dropped from the course. Damn! Only a couple days left and he was out getting into trouble, and his career was shot as well.

Nine weeks after arriving to DSS, it was finally graduation day. It was a pretty prestigious ceremony. All of us were dressed up in our Class A Uniforms. Prior to walking across the stage, as they said our names, we were handed our campaign hats. It was a well-rehearsed procedure the day prior. As we placed our new campaign hats on our heads, we would take both hands, fingers and thumbs extended and joined, and would trace them over the circular brim of the hat. After we quickly traced over the brim, our hands went down to our sides with a sharp, snapping motion. Once at the position of Attention, we would march across the stage and were handed our graduation certificates.

Most of us were skeptical about our upcoming futures on the trail. We were nervous and knew we were about to enter a changing world of working seven days a week at times and spending more time at our basic training companies than we would at home with our families.

I had a little bit more on my plate during this time that I had to get done with first. I had to get back to Fort Bragg, clear my unit and the installation, sign out on leave, and get up to Michigan (where me and the wife were from), so that she could give birth to our firstborn. At the time, she was already pushing nine months of pregnancy. After this was complete, we were to drive back to Fort Jackson, sign into the installation, find a place to live, and then I could begin my two years on the Trail. In October of 2000, I graduated from the United States Army Drill Sergeant School and was officially a Basic Combat Training Drill Sergeant for the next two years.

CHAPTER 4

DECEMBER 2000 TO DECEMBER 2002 MY TIME ON THE TRAIL

Second Battalion, 60th Infantry Regiment was my new battalion of assignment for the next two years. My starship was my place of work and my home. "Starship" is what we called the battalion area because it was shaped in a hexagon with six companies at each apex and the battalion headquarters out front. Not to mention the Army referred to them as the Basic Training Starship Barracks. They were built in the 1970s. There were eight basic training battalions at Fort Jackson in 2000.

I was assigned to Alpha Company, 4th Platoon. Alpha Gators and the 4th Platoon Mad Dawgs were my two logos that I would be living by from there on out. I reported to the First Sergeant, who introduced me to the Company Commander and then took me upstairs to our platoon bay and introduced me to the Platoon Sergeant. His official title was Platoon Sergeant, anyway; most would refer to him as the Platoon Senior Drill Sergeant, or the boss, or their friend and mentor. I preferred the friend and mentor method, and so did he; it made the environment much easier to be in. All three drill sergeants in the platoon knew who was in charge, and we also knew we had to come together as a team in order to accomplish each day's tasks. For privacy purposes, I will only use first names of personnel that I was close with on a daily basis. Some I may not remember, so I will refer to them by a nickname, or simply Drill Sergeant or DS So-and-So.

The First Sergeant left us and went back downstairs to his office. "You got any paperwork for me, like your last NCOER (Noncommissioned Officer Evaluation Report) or anything?" my new platoon sergeant asked.

"Yes, Sergeant," I replied. "Or do I call you Drill Sergeant?" I stood in front of his desk at parade rest.

He told me to sit down at the empty desk in the office, which was mine to have. He immediately went into our introduction, the way he wanted it done, not the formal military style of parade rest and handshakes. He then went into his concept of working together in this environment. "Okay, my name is Tim. I would prefer that you call me by my first name. In front of the privates, you will refer to me as Drill Sergeant So-and-So (his obvious last name). I would like to refer to you as your first name, and in front of the privates, same rule applies, unless you have a problem with that. If you do, I will call you Drill Sergeant—I can't pronounce your last name."

I said to him, "It's pronounced Aga-naga, and I'm good with the first name thing, Tim. I actually prefer 'Augi' when I'm referred to by my rank or Drill Sergeant. Aga-naga has way too many syllables, and most people just end up screwing it up anyway. So I always go by 'Sergeant Augi.'"

Tim nodded and said, "Okay, sounds good."

Tim was a staff sergeant promotable at the time and was just waiting on his sequence number to come up for promotion to E-7. As a matter of fact, during this time period, all drill sergeants were staff sergeants (E-6) and sergeants first class (E-7). There were no sergeants (E-5). The only E-4 or E-5s assigned to a BCT Company were the supply room and administrative representatives. Other than the First Sergeant, Executive Officer, and Company Commander, everybody else were drill sergeants. There were twelve total drills per company, three per platoon, with four platoons. Of course, very seldom were there three per platoon at any given time.

Back to Tim. He had come from the Special Operations community within the Army prior to getting levied for the Trail. He was Aviation Branch and previously was assigned to the 160th Special Operations Aviation Regiment (Airborne) at Fort Campbell, Kentucky. So he had more of the laid back, Special Ops mentality, and coming from the insane, fast-paced Bragg, hooha, hooha mentality, I was okay with a little calm. Make no mistake about it, though, Tim was a no-shit guy that would tell you like it was. If you were fucked up, he'd tell you in a heartbeat, especially when it came to getting the mission accomplished. Tim said, "Look, I try to find a way to make our lives (the three of us assigned to the platoon) easier amongst each other in order to get our jobs done to standard. If me calling you Nate or you calling me Tim makes our communication with each other easier, then so be it. Because the second we walk outside that door," he pointed out to the bay, "the insanity begins."

At the time, the Company was gone to the uniform issue facility, getting their class A dress uniforms issued to them. They were just finishing up White Cycle and had qualified with their assigned rifles. It seemed a little early for dress uniform issue, but it was the month of December, and they were getting ready to leave Fort Jackson for Christmas Exodus for two weeks. Tim had stayed back because he knew I would be coming in, and our other Drill Sergeant was with the platoon. Clothing issue was one of those BCT events that required minimal drill sergeant supervision for the day.

The other Drill was Christi. She had been there about two BCT cycles before me. She and Tim both had their previous plaques and pictures on the wall behind their desks, and Tim suggested to me that I put mine up because it showed the privates that I had accomplishments in the Army outside of the basic training environment. He said not to worry about it for the time being, because I had plenty of time to get all that done during Exodus. Instead, he told me to go get my official drill sergeant photo taken, which meant going to a little studio down the street from our battalion. I had to have my picture on the company wall downstairs outside. He asked me if I was married, and I said yes with a newborn at home. He then told me after I got my photo done to go ahead and go home and do whatever I needed to get done, such as unpacking or whatever. I said, "Oh no, Tim, I can come back. I'm ready to jump right in and get my feet wet a little bit."

"Don't worry about that, Bubba. You'll have plenty of time to 'get your feet wet' after Exodus. Trust me. Right now, you got here at a downtime that really only happens once a year. Take advantage of it, because when we get back off of Exodus, it's gonna be non-stop." Tim had a habit of calling his friends Bubba. He was born and raised in Kentucky and was a good ol' country boy.

I said, "Okay, sounds good. I appreciate you letting me take off, and I will see you in the morning."

He replied with, "Yep, be here at 0530, and I'll start showing you how it starts here every morning." As I started walking out of the office, Tim said, "Oh, yeah, and Nate, remember this: your success from here on out is no longer measured on how well you do but how successful they become during their nine weeks with us."

"Roger that," I said and walked out into the bay and through the doors out of the platoon area. I remember telling myself that I thought I was going to like my new boss Tim.

The next morning, I walked in, and there was a line of soldiers outside of the platoon CP. I walked in the office, and Tim was sitting at his desk filling out sick call slips. "Drill Sergeant Augi, can you break this line off and take some of these sick calls for me?" So I did and started signing their slips. Most of the sick calls were colds and congestion problems. Almost all year long in these bays, a lot of privates were sick all the time. You could not deny them sick call, only recommend that they not go and either suck it up or go back some other time after a big training event. After the last one had left, Tim told me exactly that. Right now, right before Exodus, there was nothing going on for training, so it wasn't a big deal having that many sick calls in the morning. Christi came in, and we got introduced to each other. Tim gave me a blue vest to put over my PT jacket, and we went downstairs. All drills on Fort Jackson wore a blue vest so that they could easily be identified as cadre.

It seemed pretty routine. The First Sergeant came out, received the accountability report from all four platoons, and then released the platoons to the drills to conduct PT. Tim marched the Mad Dawg Platoon outside of the starship, onto the open field to our platoon PT platform area, and immediately got them into an extended rectangular formation. That first morning, he stretched them out and took us on a little run around the block a couple times, and that was pretty much it. I was waiting for him to give me an introduction to the platoon, but that came later that evening. I guess that first morning I was eager to jump in and get ready to be a drill sergeant for the first time. Like he told me the day prior, there was plenty of time for that in the next two years.

All the other drills in the company were curious about me, and most of them came up and introduced themselves. It was pretty cool getting to know them all. There were the drills from 3rd Platoon that was right across the bay from us. The 3rd Platoon "Bushmasters" were led by Chuck. It was Drill Sergeant Chuck and Drill Sergeant Mac. Drill Sergeant Mac was funny and mouthy. She did not put up with anybody's shit, let alone the privates' bullshit. Chuck's other DS was an Infantryman who wasn't bad but a little serious about life at times. Downstairs was 1st Platoon, and I cannot remember their motto. Their Platoon Sergeant was Drill Sergeant D, who was an E-7 from Fort Bragg as well. As a matter of fact, he and I went to DSS together but were in separate platoons, so we really didn't know much about each other. His experienced drill sergeant was named Long. Drill Sergeant Long looked identical to Tiger Woods—I mean they could have passed for identical twins. He was funny and happy-go-lucky all of the time. He made time on the Trail go by easier, and he and I eventually became good friends. I think I'll refer to him throughout the rest of this as Tiger. As far as 2nd Platoon, their Platoon Sergeant was a former Special Forces NCO that didn't want to be there or have anything to do with any aspect of the program. Everyone could tell that it was a struggle for him to even be there every day. Actually, I sometimes wondered how he even graduated from DSS at times. He had a drill sergeant that was a bundle of nerves all the time. He just seemed on edge 24/7. I don't know if the Trail was taking its toll on him or if he was having marital problems or both. Anyway, these were the drills that I would be spending most of my two years with at Alpha Company, 2/60th at Fort Jackson.

All the drills called each other "Battle." This was short for "battle buddy," which was the cornerstone for all privates in the Initial Entry Training (IET) environment. A private was not allowed to go anywhere by themselves. They had to have a battle buddy with them at all times, especially when talking to any drill sergeant one on one. If that soldier did not have his or her battle buddy with them, we had to turn them away until they had one. Usually, they had the same one that they would pick from the beginning of basic training, but during training, there were times they simply had to grab whoever was around them when they needed to talk to a drill about something pressing at the time. I would quickly have to be confronted with this very soon, too. One thing I learned really quickly was a new drill sergeant better get their ass on board as fast as possible, because the BCT world doesn't wait for you to catch up. The privates damn sure don't care that you are new to the BCT world. All they see is the round brown hat, and you had better be able to answer their questions and fix their problems. Oh yeah, that's something else that was different from the School House. Nobody here ever referred to the soldiers as recruits. They were referred to by the DSs as the privates or simply soldiers.

Exodus was just a couple days away, and there literally wasn't anything to do but get the soldiers packed and make sure their class As were worn properly. Tim had asked me if I'd be okay with being late man for my first time. "Yeah, no problem. It's my turn anyway," I told him. Actually, I felt relieved that he had trusted me enough, this early of me being there, to stay until lights out by myself. What I didn't know was that I was about to be thrown in react mode as soon as Kitchen Patrol (KP) was over for the night.

There I was for the first time by myself with the Mad Dawgs. Most of them were downstairs in the formation area, sitting on the bleachers, shining their boots, and writing letters. Others were on the payphones. Lights out was 2100, if my memory serves me, and first call was at 0500. I was sitting at my desk in the office when I got a knock on the door. It was a female soldier that had just returned from KP duty, standing there with her battle buddy. "Drill Sergeant Augi, I have to talk to you about something."

I said, "Okay, c'mon in. What's going on?" She went on to tell me her story of what happened to her on KP. She had claimed that the KP Drill Sergeant had pushed her in the back in the mess hall. I immediately thought to myself, *No shit, my first night, actually my first time being alone with these soldiers, and I get thrown into a cadre abuse charge.* There was no wasting time for me. This was the shit they told us about in DSS, and I got it immediately my first week on the Trail. "Did anybody see him push you?" I asked her.

"No, Drill Sergeant, but it did happen. It was Drill Sergeant So-and-So from Bravo Company, and he had gotten mad at me because I wasn't moving fast enough for him. He yelled at me, and then he pushed me." So, before I caught myself starting to become an investigator or a barracks lawyer, I knew the first thing I needed to do was to find the blank sworn statement forms. We had a filing cabinet in the office, so I opened up the drawer that was labeled "blank forms," and bigger than shit, there were sworn statements right out front. I had her sit down at Tim's desk and her battle buddy sit down at Christie's. I had her fill out the sworn statement, and we both signed it.

Afterwards, I told her, "Okay, I'm going to take this up with Drill Sergeant Tim in the morning, and he will be getting back to you tomorrow." I hated throwing the ball in his court, but honestly, I really didn't know how this was going to work. This was a time when I actually could say that I was the new guy who didn't know enough yet. Tim knew the Drill Sergeant in question, and he had been there for over a year already and knew this Private for some time as well.

The next morning before PT, I told him about it and showed him the sworn statement on his desk. "Okay, I'll take care of it," he said to me. That was it. The subject was never spoken about again. It wasn't mentioned by Tim, the other Drill—who obviously never got into trouble because he was still there—or the soldier. It was a situation of a fire that was put out, and I never did find out how, nor did I ever ask. I'm not suggesting anything got swept under the rug, but I can say that whatever the outcome was, neither party involved had a problem with each other again. It made me feel somewhat relieved, too, because that was the point when I realized that Tim had your back and wasn't going to play the game of somebody getting into trouble because of accusations. My opinion of the whole thing after it all ended was that she was angry at that particular Drill Sergeant, accused him of abusing her, and perhaps took advantage of the situation of a brand-new Drill (me) being there that night. Perhaps she could have gotten more satisfaction from a new drill sergeant than she would have gotten from someone who already knew her and what her personality was like. Throughout my time on the Trail, I continuously witnessed some privates wanting to test the waters with the system. I believe that was my first test witnessing.

A couple of weeks went by and the privates were back from Christmas Exodus. It was somewhat chaotic in the formation area. All the drill sergeants were present, hollering at the soldiers coming back in. The impression in the company was that they went home for the holidays and got all laxy-dazy and lost all their discipline from the previous six weeks of BCT. It really wasn't, at least for the majority of them, but it was the drill sergeants' thing to get all spun up about. It was funny for me to see some of my battles in action with their privates.

"Oh, look! They just come back on in here, bebopping like they're back on the block!"

Another Drill would say something like, "Oh, yeah, just take your sweet ol' time getting into formation!"

Then you'd hear something like, "Oh, hell no! What the hell is that on your neck? Is that a damn hickey? Oh shit, drill sergeants, we got ourselves a loving man over here!"

I think the funniest one of all of us talking shit was Drill Sergeant Mac. Some of the shit that came out of her mouth, you would literally have to turn around and laugh so that you weren't seen doing it in front of the privates. It was priceless. Some of the female soldiers would come back with too much make-up on while they were in their uniforms. "You'd best take your ass upstairs and wash some of that shit off your face!" It was comical to the point that you realized that these soldiers were damned if they did and damned if they didn't. They were going to get it either way. It was the drill sergeant's way of saying, "Welcome back to basic training, privates."

The next day, we had our Blue Cycle Ceremony. Like the rest of BCT, Blue Cycle was pretty crammed with events and graduation requirements such as End of Cycle Testing (EOC), Drill & Ceremony Competition (D&C), a couple of tactical ranges, the Victory Forge Field Exercise, and the most important event of all: the final APFT. The reason I refer to this as the most important event is because if they failed, they did not graduate, and it flat out looked terrible on the cadre for failure to get a trainee in enough physical condition to pass the Army PT Test.

One thing I was beginning to notice that used to bother me, probably the most when I got on the Trail, was that there was almost a hatred of cadre among other companies. It was like the competition didn't end with the privates competing but with the drill sergeants as well. I guess at first I wasn't used to that, coming from infantry battalions in the regular Army. It wasn't like that there at all. Here, in BCT, it was a continuous sharp-shooting competition between cadre. It always happened when we were mixed together for an event, especially at the chow hall. The chow hall was a BCT experience all on its own. Talk about a chaotic environment. Go inside of a BCT chow hall sometime and you'll see the definition of a hostile environment, especially when a new drill sergeant enters, like myself.

The Dining Facility, or Mess Hall, or Chow Hall, was split up between two dining areas. There was Alpha and Bravo Companies on one side and Charlie and Delta on the other. There was one empty company area in the battalion, and that was for Foxtrot Company during the summer months, known as the "summer surge." It was a company of reserve drill sergeants that would come into Fort Jackson for two BCT cycles during the summer surge, in order to augment the battalion with the abundant number of trainees that would come in during that time period. Each company in the battalion would usually task out one drill sergeant per company to assist the reservists. Ours was Fox Company, and don't ask me why it wasn't Echo Company to fill in the correct sequence.

Getting back to the hostile crowds in the chow hall, the row of tables that were cadre only was verbally insulting at times. "Hey, Drill Sergeant, I just seen one of your privates grab a fucking soda out of the machine! It must be Candy Land over there in Alpha Company, as usual!" This is the kind of shit I was talking about that literally threw me off when I first got there. Hell, I was thinking to myself that perhaps they were allowed to have sodas during Blue Cycle, I didn't know. Come to find out, the answer was no. During my time on the Trail, we never authorized the privates to have anything other than water, milk, or juice from the chow hall. The reality was that this particular Drill Sergeant from Bravo Company was fucking with me, because I was new to the game, and he was feeling me out. I remember his face, too, but not his name. He was a Bravo Company Platoon Sergeant who had been there probably as long as Tim and Chuck. After a couple of cycles, I was cool with him, but not so much that first couple of weeks. There were a couple of other asshole drills from the other side, too, that would wander over to our area and run their mouths. That was okay. In the back of my head, I knew they didn't know where I came from, and being an asshole definitely can go both ways.

It happened again about a week later. "Hey, Drill Sergeant, one of your privates just snuck a cup of coffee from the dispenser!"

I looked around towards the last of the Bravo Company trainees and saw one Private with his boot laces out of his boots. "Hey, soldier, stand the hell up. Who is your drill sergeant?" I asked. He pointed over at the big mouth and said his name. I said, "Hey, Drill Sergeant, this Private can't even wear his uniform correctly in Blue Cycle! His damn boot laces are all over the damn floor and shit! Hell, I thought I was gonna start repelling off the sons-of-bitches! Is this your product of leadership?! Fucking weak!" I then sat down two tables down from him and started eating my breakfast. He just looked at me with a smile on his face. I never heard anymore shit talking from him again, at least not toward me anyway. As a matter of fact, he was cool with me from that point on. Years later, I had run into him at Fort Lewis, Washington, at one of the shoppetts, and we shot the shit for a few minutes. It was a small Army. I still had to shut the other drills up from the other side, and eventually down the road I would.

One morning, Tim and I were sitting around getting the soldiers' graduation packets started, at least checking through them to ensure they had the correct items in each. He was going through them and telling me what had to be in each by the time they graduated, and we sealed and sent them off to AIT with the soldier (Advanced Individual Training or their Military Occupational Service "job" training). Christie was with the soldiers out in the bay, going over barracks maintenance with them. "Hey, Bubba, I'm going to need you to pitch Inspection Arms to them this afternoon, if you're up to it."

I said, "Yeah, no problem." Tim was going to have them draw their weapons so that we could start going over Drill and Ceremony Competition sequence with them. He told me he wanted me to take that task over, marching them in the competition. I was pumped up to do it, because I happened to like doing D&C and wanted the challenge. He was going to march them this cycle and have me watch. The next cycle was going to be all mine. I asked him, "Hey, Tim, where do you want me to form them up to give the module?"

"Module? No, sir, we don't do that here. Just go through the task and teach them so that they'll understand it. Trust me, they'll get it faster, and it will make more sense to them." I was so relieved. There would be no modules during my time on the trail. Those days were over for me. Tim told me, in the most respectful way, "You're gonna find out that we do things a little different in reality here in BCT than perhaps you were taught over at that School House."

"Roger that, understood," I replied. I was still relieved. We still taught them, obviously, every single D&C movement to the set standard; we simply didn't make every single step an individual lesson. My God, how the hell would you have time in this place? I did hear that there were units on Fort Jackson that would make it mandatory for every movement. That seemed to be adding to the timeline that was already packed full.

"Nope, just line them up here in the bay and go over it with them step by step until you feel comfortable that they have it down. I already taught them all other Advanced Manual of Arms, except for Inspection Arms. Next week is the competition before Victory Forge, and I want them to be squared away," Tim instructed.

After lunch, Tim had them in formation downstairs outside of the arms room cage. He was teaching me the formalities on how they drew their weapons. He sounded off with, "In weapon number sequence . . . " The privates would sound back off with, "In weapon number sequence . . . " Then Tim finalized it with, "Count off!" The privates would all sound off with all the numbers of weapons assigned to the platoon. At the same time, they would fall out of the formation and line up at parade rest in a single file line outside of the arms room cage. Once they received their weapon, they would look down at the chamber, pull the charging handle back, release it, and place their weapon on safe. They would then fall back in at position of Attention in the formation area. Tim got in front of the formation and sounded off with, "Drill Sergeant Augi!" I ran in front of the formation, stopped, did a left face, and saluted him. Tim then told me, "They're all yours, Drill Sergeant. Take them upstairs and conduct Advanced Manual of Arms Training with them."

"Yes, Drill Sergeant," I replied. I dropped my salute, took one thirty-inch step forward, conducted an about face, and told the platoon, "On the command of Fall Out, get upstairs and toe the line with your weapons and stand by for my instructions. Fall Out!"

I had them lined up with their rifles in the platoon bay, toeing the line in front of the bunks. There was a square line painted on each bay floor of all the barracks in our company, and that was where we would have them lined up inside. "Okay, listen up. I'm going to talk you all through Inspection Arms with your assigned M16A2 rifles." Without thinking about it, I started modulating unconsciously. "Inspection arms from order arms is a seven-count movement. The command is Inspection Arms. On the command of execution, Arms, execute port arms in two counts. On the third count, move the left hand from the hand-guard of the weapon and grasp the pistol grip, thumb over the lower portion to the bolt catch." I actually caught myself and remembered what Tim told me that morning. He was right; only about half of them understood what the hell I was saying to them. So I grabbed one of the rifles and talked them through it as I did it with them. After about half an hour, they were getting it, and it was running smoother and smoother. Tim was in the office, probably evaluating whether or not I could teach them something or if I was a screamer and that's it. Nope, I was teaching, and they were learning. I was actually enjoying it until the bay door opened up.

Another Drill Sergeant from Bravo Company came in and started yelling at one of the soldiers over something. He stood in the bay as if he were evaluating me giving my class. I remember saying something about it being a seven-count movement again, and that's when it happened. He started sharp-shooting me. "No, Drill Sergeant, it's an eight-count movement."

Now I was on the spot. "No, Drill Sergeant, it's a seven-count." Then he wanted to argue with me. Mistake number one (and I was new at this, but new these simple rules), he countered my instruction. Mistake number two, he did it in front of the soldiers. Not to mention, he was flat-out wrong about it being an eight-count movement.

He said, "Listen up here, soldier, this is how it's done!" One thing I remember about him was that he never said their names; it would always come out as "dummy" in a very sarcastic manner.

The next thing I heard coming from the office was Tim. "Hey, Drill Sergeant So-and-So, I need you in here." He went in, and the door shut. That was my first impression of him in the training environment. I knew it was going to be a long road with him, and I hoped I only had to see him in the chow hall. I went back to teaching Inspection Arms by myself after Drill Sergeant Tim pulled this other Drill off the scene.

The next day, we had a surprise Health & Welfare Inspection in each of the bays. First and second platoon would conduct their inspections downstairs in their bays, and us and third platoon would do our inspections in our bays. I guess this was routine, especially since they just recently got back from Exodus. Again, I sort of sat back and observed how this was going to play out. It was exactly what I expected, too. Wall lockers were getting pillaged through, drill sergeants climbing up on bunks in order to look inside of the ceiling tiles with flashlights and looking through the latrines. I don't know what it was, but the privates always thought they could hide stuff in their long dress coats. That first inspection, we found like three cans of chewing tobacco, a Walkman radio, and no shit, Drill Sergeant Mac found a cellular phone. Remember, this was in 2000. Cell phones were definitely not a thing yet. "Oh hell, NO! What the hell is this? A mobile phone? What is this for, so you can get booty calls in the middle of the night?" It happened to be a female soldier that had it hidden in the ceiling tile above her bunk. It was nice, too, with a leather case and everything. There it sat on the desk in the front of the bay. Punishments for contraband at this point were loss of phone privileges for the rest of basic training. It may not seem a lot to the average person, but in this environment, phone privileges meant everything to a basic trainee.

It was also Army Values Training time for the final values class for these soldiers' journey through BCT. Army Basic Training used to be eight weeks. That's what it was when I went through ten years prior. The Army added an additional week for values training. The seven Army Values were the acronym LDRSHIP, which stood for Loyalty, Duty, Respect, Selfless Service, Honor, Integrity, and Personal Courage. The last class that Tim was about to present was Personal Courage. He had the platoon sit around the desk in front of the platoon bay. We had a butcher block tablet set up with all the Army Values, and he reviewed quickly each of the previous six, then he went into the final one. It was interesting watching him teach it, because he turned it into a final class of the light at the end of the tunnel for them in order to gain their interest. He had a way of making them get interested in non-interesting subjects. For each Values class, we gave them the Army definition and then would have them give us examples and then would compare the value towards upcoming training events that they were about to execute during that week of training. Tim used Personal Courage as an example of our upcoming ranges for the next week, such as Hand Grenades, U.S. Weapons, the Night Infiltration Course (NIC), and the Victory Forge Field Exercise.

The next week was busy, busy, busy, and we were on the go. All the ranges I just mentioned, the D&C Competition, and the End of Cycle Testing (EOC). EOC was an entire day event for first aid, communications, Nuclear Biological Chemical (NBC), map reading, etc. Pretty much we were going over all soldier skills testing. The soldiers were definitely under the stress of passing all these events. Other company drill sergeants would test our soldiers on these events, and we would do the same for theirs as well. For us, it was mainly Bravo Company that tested our soldiers. If your platoon won any of these events that were graded and/or judged at battalion level, you would be awarded a streamer to place on your platoon's guide-on. It was competition, and it meant a lot to us also. It was a rite of passage to talk shit to others within the company and the battalion. We would say shit like, "Our Platoon's guide-on has so many streamers, we're gonna need two privates to carry it." The soldiers loved it, and I'm not going to lie, the drill sergeants had pride in it, too. It was a mark to show how much your training paid off and the quality of your platoon.

Out of all the ranges for BCT, the hand grenade range always had us a little nervous. After all, these were new trainees throwing two live grenades, which was also mandatory for graduation of BCT. The range cadre at hand grenades truly earned their pay. I believe during my two years on the Trail there were two separate incidences where the range cadre had to grab a private and throw them and themselves over the berm from a live high explosive grenade being dropped by accident. Of course, the soldiers spent half the morning at the practice portion of the range, and they had to certify with practice grenades before they could go over to throw live. It definitely was a little bit more of a tense range than the others.

It was my first Victory Forge Field Exercise and another great learning experience. Tim broke it down to me right off the bat. He made sure I understood that this was basic training, not the 82nd Airborne Division, and not to get too spun up if this wasn't field training like we were used to in the active Army. I understood and had no problem with it being more laid back. Victory Forge was about a three-night field exercise, and on the fourth evening, right before dark, we took off for a ten- to twelve-mile foot march back to the battalion.

The soldiers would dig foxholes to standard so that we had a company defensive perimeter. They would man these positions with their battle buddies. We taught them to always improve their positions with camouflage and constantly fortify them to make them stronger. Some were actually impressive. If these privates got anything out of Victory Forge, it was how to build a two-man fighting position according to Army standard.

Once the perimeter was generally set with minor fortifications, we took the soldiers out and taught them some basic patrolling, such as conducting a reconnaissance (Recon), ambush, and a platoon attack. It was good, old fashioned Army training. We also got them introduced to some great Army terms, such as, "If it ain't raining, we ain't training!" Also, "It doesn't rain in the Army, soldiers, it rains on the Army!" They seemed to get a kick out of it. As far as having enemy personnel to play the opposing force (OPFOR), or the enemy forces, we would get our own cadre. Maybe our supply guys and/or administrative NCO, with a couple of drill sergeants to run around and pop off a few blank rounds at the soldiers. We coordinated all operations over our radios whenever we wanted them to hit the trainees. We made it as real and as exciting as we could with the equipment we had. I used to get them spun up by going from hole to hole and telling them stuff like, "Whoa, what is that out there, soldier? You guys better get ready. I think they're gonna hit us any time now." They would get all into it and have their weapons at the ready.

We would finish off the field exercise with a grand finale firefight in the defensive perimeter. We'd throw smoke grenades and maybe even a CS gas grenade (riot control gas) or two, since they had their protective masks on them at all times. After it was all over, we would have them conduct an extensive police call of the entire training area. They filled in their fighting positions and picked up all the brass from their blank rounds. In between events for that finale day out in the field, we would show them how to clean their weapons in the field by breaking down the upper receivers and wiping the bolt carriers down, getting all the dirt and sand off of them. "Do not, for the love of God, break down your bolts!" We preached that to them, in the event they would lose a small piece of their weapon, such as one of the pins in the bolt assembly group, while we were in the field.

The final foot march out of Victory Forge was a pretty big deal in BCT. It was a mandatory event for graduation, and it ended with the Victory Forge Ceremony back at the battalion. The march was a long, straightaway movement conducted in the hours of darkness. Like I said, it was between a ten- to twelve-mile road march with all their equipment, which included a thirty-five-pound rucksack, with their helmets on and weapons at the ready. We stopped them along the range road approximately two, possibly three, times, depending on the heat index, for water breaks along the way. The pace was relatively slow due to us preventing heat casualties among these new trainees. Their bodies were not used to conducting a fast-paced forced foot march in the South Carolina heat, especially when it was during the summer surge. Although some of them physically could if we had pushed them to.

Once we got to the end of the road march, outside of the battalion area, we halted everybody, got them some more water, and had them get their composures back. The First Sergeant got on his radio with the Battalion S-3 (Operations) NCO. Once they were ready for us, we formed our companies up and marched them over to the Battalion Headquarters, where they had a large bonfire lit up and burning. We formed all companies in the front of Headquarters 2/60th and received a speech from the Battalion Commander. He congratulated the soldiers for completing all major events of basic combat training and told them that they were well on their way towards graduation in a little over a week. He then commanded each company to issue each soldier their Values Tag. We opened ranks within the company, and all drill sergeants went through and issued their soldiers their tags. These Values tags were to be placed on their identification tags or dog tag chains. It was a pretty important event of BCT prior to finishing up a cycle.

The only two major events left on the calendar were the Battalion Final Inspection and the Final APFT. For the final inspection preparation, all equipment, including each soldier's tactical gear, weapon, wall locker, and barracks as a whole, would be inspected by the Battalion Commander and Command Sergeant Major. Us drill sergeants would take our own money and purchase mass amounts of shaving cream and the spray canned air for weapons cleaning. Tim even brought in a couple of power drills to rod through the barrels of the M16s with metal brushes. We would spend about three full days preparing for the inspection. Tim taught me to break it down in phases. Day one, get all the equipment cleaned, and while it was drying, start on the weapons. The bay cleaning should be held for last. We had the latrines so clean you could have literally eaten off the floors.

The final Army Physical Fitness Test was graded by Bravo Company drill sergeants, and we graded their soldiers in return. It turned into drama at times, like everything else in this environment. You'd see drill sergeants bringing them out coffee; some would even have breakfast muffins or Krispy Kreme donuts for the other drill sergeants. It got to the point where I would see straight-up ass kissing from one company to another over a PT Test. I guess in the reality of it, every soldier had to pass to graduate, and some thought that those soldiers that were on the edge of failure were in the hands of these other drills. I didn't kiss any of their asses. As a matter of fact, I wouldn't even talk to them. I had a mentality of "do your job." I didn't need to kiss their asses for them to do their jobs to standard. I'd be damned if I ever offered those Bravo Company assholes any cups of coffee. I'm telling you, they rubbed me the wrong way from the beginning. The reality of it was if any of my trainees failed the

APFT, they're going to get retested by somebody else. So I wasn't kissing anybody's ass.

I missed my first sequence of graduation events, which were the rehearsal, family day, and graduation itself. I got tasked that final week of the cycle to become the company primary hand-to-hand combat or unarmed combat instructor. There was a week-long class at Fort Jackson that we had to receive and get certified through. A team from Fort Benning came up and taught us classes on the new Brazilian Jiu Jitsu style hand-to-hand fighting techniques that the Army was changing over to. It was pretty intense. I actually broke a finger during the training. Who knew? My first broken bone in the Army and it was done being a drill sergeant at Fort Jackson, SC.

My first full basic training cycle was pretty chaotic, as all are. One drill sergeant per platoon usually went over to the Replacement Battalion to pick up the new soldiers. The unwritten rule was that we did not interfere with or yell at the new trainees while they were still under the control of the Replacement Drill Sergeants. This was going to be my first full basic training cycle, and Tim wanted me there for the whole thing, including Replacement pick up, in order to get the full experience. This I can still remember as if it were yesterday. It was Drill Sergeant Mac, Tiger Woods, me, and the Platoon Sergeant from 2nd Platoon.

You would have thought that this group of privates were best friends with their current drill sergeants they had from Replacement. I mean, they weren't even referring to them as drill sergeant. "Oh yeah, that's cool," was how they were talking to one another. On this subject, I am going out on a limb and am going to go ahead and say this now. A drill sergeant during my time on the trail used to receive an additional $275 per month for Special Duty Pay by the Army. I'm sure it was supposed to be in accordance with working seven days a week, along with the daily hours that went with it, especially the first three to five weeks. Replacement and AIT Drill Sergeants received the same extra pay as well. These particular drills should not receive

$275 or whatever the pay is today for Special Duty Pay. This isn't just my opinion but that of almost any other BCT Drill Sergeant out there. Replacement and AIT Drills are not with the soldiers twenty-four seven, seven days a week. Especially AIT Drills that usually do PT with the trainees and then march them off to their MOS Training NCOs that have the soldiers all day. There are separate cadre that teach them Monday through Fridays on their specific MOS training. It is not the responsibility of the drill sergeants, as it is in the BCT environment.

A Replacement Drill Sergeant's number one job is to get the new soldiers in-processed into the installation and to ensure they can run a mile without passing out before they can send them to us. In actuality, most Replacement Drills used to be BCT DSs anyway and would probably agree with not receiving the additional pay. Most of them volunteer for a third year on Fort Jackson for whatever reason, such as children in school, other family reasons, or they simply do not wish to go back to the regular Army to do their jobs right away.

I remember telling Mac, "These soldiers seem to be a little close to these drills over here."

She replied with, "Oh yeah, Augi, we see this every time we come over here at the beginning of a cycle. When you hear the term 'candy land,' this is where it really is, Battle. Don't worry about it. I know it's hard to watch this shit and keep your mouth shut, but that shit's about to end real quick, Battle," she said to me with sarcasm in her voice. She leaned into me and told me to keep quiet on the bus ride back to the battalion, too, wait until we told them to get off the buses and then all hell would break loose on them.

I honestly couldn't wait, because the way they were acting and were allowed to act with these drills was making me more pissed by the minute. It took me back to when I went through basic training ten years earlier. I remember as well that the Replacement Drills were more laid back than the BCT Drills, because when we got off the cattle trucks from Replacement to our BCT Battalion, it was pure chaos. That feeling always sticks with any soldier, even us drill sergeants that were about to instill the same shock factor here in the next hour or so. We just stood off to the side until they began loading on the buses.

On the way to the battalion, we had them place their heads down on their duffle bags that were on their laps. We gave them specific instructions not to talk to one another and not to look outside the windows, just keep their heads down in the duffle bags. They were still acting all lazy-dazy for the bus ride over. Once the buses stopped in front of the battalion, I asked them politely to look up at me. They did. I then asked them to do me a favor.

I remember Drill Sergeant Mac saying, "Do me a favor?"

I then said to them, "Get your fucking asses off this fucking bus now, goddamn it! Move your sorry asses, privates! Get the fuck off the bus!"

All the other company drills were outside the starship hollering at them to hurry up and move. It was utter chaos at the time, soldiers dropping their bags, mass confusion, and some crying as well. We put as much stress onto them as anybody could think of. We did everything but place our hands on them, of course.

Once in the company formation area, we had them drop their bags and move to the bleachers. It was quick and fast, not too formal of a class, but fast and furious. We had them line up in a single file line and file into the bleachers from top to bottom, yelling at them the entire time. "Who the fuck told you to sit down, soldiers?! Stand your sorry asses up until you're told to sit down!" Once all the soldiers were in the bleachers, one of us gave them the command, "Take Seats!" The Company Commander and the First Sergeant then came out and gave them their introduction into basic training and introduced each drill sergeant to the entire two hundred fifty–soldier company.

Once the introductions were complete and the First Sergeant turned the company back over to the drills, we had to form them up by platoon and get them into dinner chow before we got them upstairs to the bays. Forming up, marching to, and getting into line in the mess hall was a task by itself in the BCT environment. One drill sergeant per platoon would have to move up and be present at the podium in the entrance of the mess hall in order to take head count. There were three separate pages that needed to be recorded. Active Duty, Reserve, and National Guard had three separate sheets. Each soldier was to sound off with, "Drill Sergeant, Active Duty, 7249, Drill Sergeant!" "7249" was the example of giving their last four of their social security number, which was what the drill sergeant had to write down on the correct component sheet. As soon as the soldier was through sounding off with their last four, the next soldier would sound off with his or hers.

It got pretty intense inside that walkway, especially when you had drill sergeants screaming the whole time they were in there. The head count Drill couldn't even hear the trainee and had to tell them to sound off again. Once the cycle got going a few days, and the soldiers were used to this pattern, the Charge of Quarters (CQ) Drill Sergeant would do the head count for his entire company. Male drills were responsible for CQ duties throughout the entire battalion, and females did the Battalion Staff Duty. There was a reason for this. No male drill sergeant could enter a female bay after lights out; they needed to be escorted by a female drill for headcount purposes twice throughout each night.

Once the entire platoon was in the dining portion of the mess hall, the last soldier for that platoon would sound off with, for example, "Drill Sergeant, last Mad Dawg seated, Drill Sergeant!" From that point, they had seven minutes to eat and start heading out to formation. No talking, no looking around, head and eyes on their trays of food, and that was it. When their seven minutes was up, we'd say, "That's it, you're done with chow. Get up and get out in formation—move your asses!" Actually, it was only the last soldier that was timed for the seven-minute period. The platoon did not have to wait on him or her to sit. Once they sat down, no matter what order they were, they could begin eating. Only the last trainee was timed after they sat down to get out of the dining facility.

Once back in the company area, we had them fall back on their bags, grab them, and head upstairs to the platoon bays. The first thing we showed them was toeing the line painted on the floor. "Every time we tell you to get upstairs and toe the line, this is exactly what you will do, Mad Dawgs! Understood?"

All answered, "Yes, Drill Sergeant!"

We then had them dump their duffle bags on the floor. Immediately, we conducted basic clothing issue inspection. This is pretty routine for all basic training in all branches of service. The drill sergeant calls out each item of clothing, and the private holds it up above his or her head. The other drill sergeants would walk down the line, and once we saw the item of clothing, we would tell them to pack it back up in their duffle bag. "Don't be getting your shit mixed up with your buddy next to you, because if you screw this up, soldiers, you're going to dump them and start all over. It doesn't matter to us what time you get to bed tonight. Either way, first call tomorrow morning is still at 0500. It doesn't matter to us how much sleep you get!"

This went on for the next eight weeks, and then again, and again, and again. I went through eleven basic training cycles in two years, after which I was so on edge the rest of my military career. I still am today, but not as bad as when I first got out ten years ago. Like I said, I still get woken up by the wife all the time for cursing and screaming at soldiers in my sleep. I don't think it'll ever go away.

One thing that was forever engrained in my mind during my time on the Trail was my individual experience of what happened to our country on September 11, 2001. Everybody always has their personal time or experience of what they were doing or where they were at during that horrific morning, right? Mine was being a drill sergeant on Fort Jackson, South Carolina. September 11, 2001, was actually the day before one of our graduations for that particular cycle. The soldiers were to graduate the next morning and move on to their advanced individual training elsewhere. What a horrific morning, especially before 10:00 a.m. on that fucking morning.

We were conducting graduation rehearsal for the next morning of this particular cycle. We were right in the middle of our rehearsal when, all of a sudden, we were ordered to report to the front of the parade field. "All cadre immediately stop all procedures and report to the bleachers for a mandatory briefing by the Battalion Commander." We really didn't think anything of it, other than it was sort of unusual to stop us from conducting a rehearsal for graduation that was happening the next morning, but whatever. It must have been something important. Man, it was definitely important.

What I heard from the Battalion Commander's mouth was an ever-lasting change of our lives. Not only to us as servicemembers, but to the country as a whole. "Company commanders and drill sergeants, there has been a terrorist attack in New York City. Two civilian airline aircraft have flown into the two Twin Towers of the World Trade Center in Manhattan. Our orders are to cease all training and immediately return to our battalion and inform these soldiers. All soldiers that are from New York and/or have parents or any family member that lives and works in Manhattan are to call home immediately. Understand?"

We all replied, "Yes, sir."

When I climbed into Tim's truck with him to head back after the soldiers got on the buses, he had the radio on. It was live radio when we heard that a third plane had crashed into the Pentagon in our nation's capital. Tim immediately put his truck into park. He looked at me, and in the most serious voice I ever heard him speak, he said, "Hey, Nate, our country is under attack . . . " I never forgot that tone or that statement he made to me. As I write this now, I have goosebumps on my arms. I'm not bullshitting you.

When we got back to the battalion, we had the soldiers call home, and drill sergeants that were from New York called home as well. Honestly, there was only a small number of soldiers that needed to call home. Actually, I told all the soldiers to call home, because this was something that was so emotionally devastating to all people, not just the military, but all human beings across the globe.

None of us could go home that afternoon, as we would be able to regularly. Actually, the day before graduation day in this environment was usually the earliest days to go home to our families, but September 11, 2001, was not. I remember thinking to myself that on that day, our way of life had just changed forever—at least for the rest of my life on this earth. I remember thinking that at this point, I wished I was back on Fort Bragg, in the 82nd Airborne Division, because I knew they were going straight to Afghanistan to kick Al Qaeda's ass, and they did just that. I wanted to be part of it, and not be stuck at Fort Jackson, South Carolina, as a Basic Training Drill Sergeant. Don't worry, I had my chances to fight this Global War on Terrorism, as the first chapter and the next couple of chapters explain in this book.

CHAPTER 5

2008-2009
KADHIMIYA DISTRICT
NORTHWEST BAGHDAD

In December 2008, around a day or two after Christmas, a car bomb killed at least twenty-four innocent civilians that wanted to worship at the Al-Kadhimiya Mosque. The savage car bomber also severely wounded forty-six others. Many of these worshipers were Shiite pilgrims. The explosion occurred about one hundred yards from Bab al-Dirwaza, one of the main gates to the mosque. This occurred in our sector of responsibility and was one of the most horrific terrorist attacks not only in Baghdad for that year, but during our battalion's deployment to Iraq.

It was referred and defined as sectarian violence that has existed in this country and throughout the Middle East between the Sunni and the Shia Muslims for decades and even centuries. I haven't even got into the Kurdish population to the north, but that's another story for another day.

This was the reality of the Global War on Terrorism. Actually, I should say "is" the reality, because it is still ongoing and probably always will be, at least for the rest of my time on this planet. I've said this and believe this still to this day. To all my fellow servicemembers past and present, please don't take this the wrong way. I know there were many other dangerous areas in the Middle East during this time period; this is my opinion, and I'm sure that of many others as well. But if anybody served in the city of Baghdad, Iraq, between 2006 and 2008, you were in the most dangerous city and combat area in the world.

My last two years in the Army, I got stationed at Fort Riley, Kansas. I was assigned to the 1st Battalion, 18th Infantry Regiment. They were a combined arms battalion with a headquarters company, two companies of mechanized infantry, and two armored companies. We were part of the 2nd Heavy Brigade Combat Team, 1st Infantry Division. I was a master sergeant and was hoping to get assigned as a company first sergeant. Instead, I was sent to the Battalion S-3 Shop as the Operations Noncommissioned Officer in Charge (NCOIC), responsible for managing all the staff in the shop. All five of the company first sergeant positions had just been filled prior to my arrival at Fort Riley. Apparently, I arrived a month or two too late. Oh well, that's the way the Army goes. Either way, I was planning on hitting my twenty-year mark and retiring anyway, as I talked about at the end of *Division*.

Our brigade was scheduled to deploy to Iraq for a year approximately four or five months after I arrived. It was a great unit with awesome leadership. I got along with all of the soldiers, the staff, and all the companies' leadership as well. They all welcomed me with open arms, and it was a tight unit. I believe there were just a very small handful of leaders in this battalion that already hadn't been to Iraq once or twice already.

It was sort of a chilling time to go to Iraq, especially the area we were heading to in Northwest Baghdad. Don't get me wrong—not that any time was a good time to go to war over there, but this particular time seemed especially tense. The 2007 surge had just finished up, which was a success for U.S.-led coalition forces. It was a major defeat for Al Qaeda pretty much all over the city of Baghdad. The shit was getting out of hand with their tactics. I'm talking straight evil. Just so you the reader can get a more detailed understanding of what kind of animals we were facing over there, I'll relay to you an example. In February of 2008, in central Baghdad, Al Qaeda terrorists strapped explosives to two women with Down's syndrome and detonated them in the middle of a market, killing forty-six innocent people and injuring one hundred more. So, when you hear the term "savages" from me, you can completely understand where I'm coming from. These individuals had no concern for human life at all.

Our battalion was headquartered at Forward Operating Base Justice in the heart of the Kadhimiya District of Baghdad. It was adjacent to the Tigris River, and on the other side was Sadr City. Sadr City was very significant for some of the leaders in our battalion. They were part of many battles during their time there in 2006. So it was specifically eerie for them to be back in this area of the city. Actually, it was eerie for all of us, especially when it was our second or third time in this area of the world.

Being at FOB Justice was significant by itself because it was the location where Saddam Hussein was executed. Actually, there had been many executions at this base, since it was a former intelligence and law enforcement headquarters of Saddam's regime. Honestly, for most of us that stayed there, we believed the damn place was haunted as well. We relieved a battalion from the 101st Airborne Division, and their soldiers used to tell us stories of hearing people in the middle of the night screaming down the hallways. Something else creepy they told us was about the heavy-duty woodchipper that they had just gotten rid of prior to our arrival to relieve them. It was out back of the headquarters. The rumor was that the leaders at the camp during Saddam's era would put prisoners in it and their remains would get shot out into the Tigris River. That ought to give you goosebumps. It did me again when I was writing this.

When we first arrived there, my roommate and buddy Danny and I got assigned to our trailer that was out on the back-forty. We had to stay out back there for a week or so until the unit we were replacing started leaving, which wasn't too far away at the time. Once space was available inside the headquarters building that we would be working out of, we could move into one of the rooms inside. I can remember him and me going outside that first night to smoke a cigarette, and we were creeped out because it was just about dusk and you could hear the Muslim prayer songs over the nearby city speakers. Not to mention Sadr City being across the river was where Danny was when he was a platoon sergeant. So he was really on edge that first week. The smell of that place reminded both of us that we were back and that we were going to be there a whole year. It wasn't a comfortable feeling.

Our battalion was spread out throughout this area of Baghdad with our companies out in the communities at joint security stations (JSS), where they were mirrored up with a company of Iraqi Army or other Iraqi security forces. The point was to have our troops out living in the sectors instead of having them returning to and from the FOBs every day, the way we used to operate back in the day. It was more of a concept to have our troops not only have a show of force but live out in the communities to ensure more of a sense of trust with the locals as well.

Getting back to the creepiness of FOB Justice, there were times we would be sitting in operations and our weapons would fall over by themselves. Not once or even twice, but almost on a weekly basis. We would keep them stacked up in line on a particular wall, and they would simply fall over to one direction on their own. At first, when we first got there in September, we simply thought a breeze was coming in, causing them to fall over. The 101st guys warned us that it would happen all the time, again and again, that this place was haunted. It got to the point that we started laying them on the floor, because they were constantly getting knocked over by something all of the time. Anybody that served in our battalion tactical operations center (TOC) would agree to this.

There were a few nights as well that we would hear screams down the hallways. One night, I was awakened by a scream. When I opened the door to my room, I walked out to the hallway, and other soldiers were looking out their doors also. "What the fuck was that?" I asked.

"I know, Sergeant Augi. I keep hearing it, too. It's somebody fucking screaming, and it's creeping me out. I heard they used to torture people in this place back in the day."

I shut my door and laid back down until I fell back asleep, which I did. A few minutes later, somebody began knocking on my door. I got up, walked over to it, and opened it. It was the soldier that handed me the jawbone in Iraq before. He said, "Here you go, Sergeant. I found this in the hallway and figured you wanted it."

I sat up in bed and realized it was another bad dream. I put my hands over my face and said, "Please, God, make this stop." I was too afraid to go back to sleep, so I woke up, brushed my teeth, shaved, got dressed, and went back to the TOC to go to work. I did this often so that I wouldn't be alone in my room. I'd walk into the TOC, and the Operations Sergeant Major would ask me why I was there because it wasn't my shift. He and I would switch off and on. I simply would tell him that I couldn't sleep. I went out back and lit up a cigarette. Across the river, in the distance, I could hear the gunfire exchange. I wondered who was shooting up who. Every now and again, we'd hear mortar attacks or bombs going off over there. Sadr City was a hot mess and had been that way for at least two years up to this point.

Tensions were getting extremely high in the TOC, almost comparable to having cabin fever or something like that. The Operations Sergeant Major came in one morning and started going off on one of our battle captains, which happened to be my roommate and buddy Danny—Sergeant First Class P. Danny happened to be using his chair, but much more important, a car bomb had just gone off in our sector, which killed over twenty people and wounded several more. Danny was trying to report it to the Battalion Commander, who was out in sector at the time. The Sergeant Major kept on interrupting him over his fucking chair. I saw what was coming next. Danny picked up the chair and threw it across the TOC. "There's your fucking chair, you motherfucker!" He then stormed out and left.

"Sergeant Augi, go get your boy and get his ass back in here," the Sergeant Major tried to order me.

"You go get him, Sergeant Major. That's your mess."

"I'm going to tell you one more time to go get his sorry ass, Sergeant!"

"Fuck no, leave him alone, Sergeant Major! Just let the shit cool down. He'll be fucking back, trust me." He came back, but with the Command Sergeant Major. I don't know what he said to the Operations Sergeant Major, but I don't think it was pretty. He left, and we didn't see him for the rest of the day. I was fucking pissed off. We just had a bomb go off, people were dead and wounded, and this motherfucker wanted to get shit started over a fucking chair. Good for Danny! I didn't say it, but I was glad he threw the chair. He made his point.

Back in the war, death squad–style killings in Iraq were taking place in a variety of ways. Kidnappings, followed by often extreme torture, such as using drills to drill holes in people's feet, along with execution-style killings, were becoming popular among the Shiite. Some of these killings were often public as well. In some cases, beheadings emerged as another tactic by these monsters. It wasn't uncommon for tapes of the executions to be distributed for propaganda purposes. The bodies were usually dumped on a roadside or in other places, several at a time. Some of these death squads also included members of the security forces, who killed Sunnis to avenge the consequences of the insurgency against the Shiite-dominated government.

At the end, what I and many realized with the sectarian violence between these two major tribes of the Muslim religion in Iraq, particularly in its capital of Baghdad, was that it was obviously about dominance of the areas and regions. However, there was always one thing in the way of this civil war, at least since 2003—the United States presence there. That's a fact that some may argue as an opinion, but I agree with. In my professional opinion, as an almost fifty-year-old man who's been there three times, we were and are never going to change the civil war of those two versions of that religion in that region of the world. The nation-building mentality of our current democratic government system in that particular region of the world was and will continue to be an utterly failed concept that will continue, probably for our lifetime and perhaps eternity of the human race. Who knows, right? We can hope for peace over there, but it is beyond our nation's views on government, that has made the U.S. the strongest, freest, biggest economic success in the history of this world. The governments of the Sunni, Shia, and Kurds are going to have to figure it out for themselves, and God I hope someday they will, but I am and continue to remain very skeptical of a positive result.

So that the average civilian reading this can understand what I am talking about from a different perspective, imagine a suicide bomber that so happens to be Lutheran or Baptist walking into a Catholic Mass anywhere in the United States and blowing themselves up because one believes their beliefs are more dominant than the other. They both agree that Jesus is our Messiah but disagree with the teachings on why and how. Imagine they would be willing to kill themselves and dozens or even hundreds of the other faith, which is close to the same. The Sunnis and Shia both believe that Allah is their God from the Old Testament from the Bible but disagree on Mohammad's teachings from their version of the New Testament. That's the difference, and the two are willing, and in some extreme cases are sworn, to kill each other over it. The fucked-up part is that the Kurdish to the north are hated by both, so for centuries they have been considered the outcast of the entire region, not just in Iraq, but in surrounding nations as well. This sectarian violence in Northwest Baghdad, on our battalion's deployment in 2008, cost two of our young soldiers who were both honorable squad leaders their legs—literally. One soldier was from Alpha Company and one from Bravo. They were both hit with EFPs—explosively formed penetrators, which were IEDs created by Iranian-led leadership (Shiite). These projectiles could penetrate any armored vehicle. God bless those two boys and their families for eternity . . .

There were two significant points of our battalion's deployment to Iraq in 2008. First, we were the cornerstone of acting on and complying with the Iraq Status of Forces Agreement (SOFA). This was the agreement between the United States and the Republic of Iraq on the withdrawal of the U.S. forces from Iraq. It established that U.S. combat forces would withdraw from Iraqi cities by the end of June 2009, and our battalion did just that. In the summer of 2009, our battalion left FOB Justice and re-flagged down at the Victory Base Complex. This was a huge complex of U.S. and Coalition Forces adjacent to the Baghdad International Airport. That place had everything, including a large post exchange and, more importantly, a Pizza Hut and Taco Bell. I could not believe how big that post had gotten since I left out of there before in 2004.

The other and most important significant reality of our battalion's deployment to Iraq was that we had zero killed in action, which I consider to this day to be a complete miracle. Seriously, for an infantry battalion to deploy to Operation Iraqi Freedom for an entire year without any deaths is a miracle. I said that during my speeches prior to leaving Fort Riley upon my retirement from the Army. In October of 2009, our battalion left Iraq, and our combat deployment ended. Back at Fort Riley, we had our welcome home ceremony, and the two wounded sergeants were back from Walter Reed Hospital and were able to attend. It brought tears to our eyes to see them walk across the gymnasium. They both had their prosthetic legs and were walking well with them. It was an honor to have them at our return ceremony. It was also an honor for me to have served in the Vanguard Battalion.

I was treated so well upon my retirement. The Battalion Commander, Lieutenant Colonel V, and Command Sergeant Major E made sure that not only did I receive a retirement award, but also, and most importantly to me, I was awarded the Order of Saint Maurice as well. It is an honor given to soldiers who have served in the infantry community with distinction. I still display mine proudly on my wall at home. On August 1, 2010, I retired from the United States Army with twenty years of service to this great nation.

CHAPTER 6

WAKE UP—LIVING WITH SOMEONE WHO HAS PTSD

A Testimonial From Jessica Aguinaga, Nathan's Wife

I myself do not suffer from having Post-Traumatic Stress Disorder—I can honestly say that I haven't been in any situations during my existence that would warrant having it—but I have dealt with those afflicted by PTSD my whole life. More specifically, I have dealt with many people, very close to me, who had war-induced PTSD. Before I could even understand what it was, I was already maneuvering around it.

My father is a Vietnam veteran, having served in the Brown Water Navy in Vietnam from December 1969 to June 1971. When I was young, I understood that my father was in the service and had been in war. I had a nominal understanding at that time of what he did as a job over there, had seen the pictures of him on the boats in the rivers, and I felt that his involvement in the war after volunteering was something very extraordinary. I would brag to others about his patriotism and contribution in the effort. I even knew a few of his anecdotal stories that were acceptable for children to hear. Many of his stories he didn't disclose to me personally until I was older and in the service myself, and I'm sure he has several accounts that he will avoid divulging to anyone.

My family used to go to events like fairs, rifle clubs, and the Cleveland Sportsman Show every year, and there were usually Vietnam veteran organizations with stands advocating their groups at these places. My dad always stopped and without hesitation or introduction would shake the veterans' hands, and they would say, "Welcome home," to each other. Sometimes this gesture even involved a quick man hug, which I was not used to seeing him do otherwise, but it was always an intimate moment where the two of them just knew something about each other that the rest of us, even being family, could never understand about them. Then they would commence small talk about what they did over there. They usually stuck to just job descriptions and cities they had had missions in or based out of. They were careful to leave out key elements of their personal accounts, more than likely to spare us kids and wives standing to the side watching this reunion of sorts of having to hear the sordid details.

My dad has oddities about him that I would say he picked up from the war. For one, he has a tattoo of a dagger with a ribbon around it that reads "death before dishonor." I have seen other Vietnam veterans with similar tattoos (some with the dagger stabbing through a rose or a skull) and that exact phrase, sort of a credo amongst them. Another idiosyncrasy was sleeping on his back straight as a board with his arms crossed over his chest. This was how he'd have to sleep on the boats when he had time to catch a catnap. It was also understood that when he was sleeping, we were not to bother or startle him by shaking him, rather just say his name from a distance until he woke up. I never saw him lash out in his sleep, I'm not sure if my mother ever did or not, but I believe it was more for his sake and to prevent him from having a possible episode. I did hear stories from other friends about their fathers who were Vietnam veterans where they startled them from sleep with an equally startling reaction from them, and I never tested those waters with my father. Another peculiar norm for my father is that he always sleeps with a nightlight on, still to this day, and if he has to travel, he will take one with him. I guess when you have woken up in a war zone in the past, you want to know exactly where you are in the present when you wake up.

My brother is also a war veteran who served in Iraq. I noticed differences when he came home, such as being more emotional. He has always been caring, but he seems to become easily distressed since he came home and is typically overly distraught by serious situations, such as family becoming ill or someone else he knows going through a hard time, things he has no control over and that didn't spin him up as much before he left. Also when he first got back, loud, abrupt noises really bothered him, such as metal on metal, cars backfiring, and even though he was able to mentally prepare himself for 4th of July fireworks, he was not comfortable with them, even after deciding to stay in the house during the show. Some of these triggers have lightened up over time for him.

One of my dearest friends went to Iraq twice. She and I were stationed in Germany together and were inseparable for the most part. She, too, had issues when she first got back home. She would get agitated with civilians quickly, and she had issues with crowds. She came to visit me once in college after she had just come back home, and we went to a local bar, something we had done dozens of times together, but when she got back, it was different, and she asked if we could leave the scene and just hang out in my apartment. She was apologetic and kept saying she didn't know what was wrong with her, that she used to love going out, but I knew what it was and didn't blame her for it, and for her, this apprehension of being out in public seems to have lighted up with time as well.

For these veterans, though, I think the issues just seem to have subsided for those of us around them because they learn how to project normalcy for the rest of our sakes as much as possible. Not just for the rest of us but to spare themselves the annoyance of having to explain themselves to people. When you are with a person who has PTSD, you learn their triggers and work around them like a planet orbiting the sun. So with this person, maybe you do things that don't involve crowds or skip on 4th of July fireworks or don't touch them to wake them up. Another common veteran trait is having to face the doorway in a restaurant, so maybe you concede to sitting on the other side automatically to accommodate them, knowing your meal will be more enjoyable if you can put this one trigger at ease. These are things you do after time without even thinking about them when you love someone with PTSD. Having this previous experience, I think, better equipped me for beginning my relationship with my husband, a three-time combat veteran, but I've come to find every person is different in what their PTSD entails, and there is a learning curve in every case.

Nate and I met while he was on active duty and I was in the National Guard. I knew he had been to combat, and I also knew that he wouldn't be without some issues from it, especially having been Infantry in the 82nd Airborne Division. Those soldiers saw some serious action in the years he was there. Like I said, I am not a combat veteran, and there is almost a kind of survivor's remorse to that. You know you cannot truly empathize with those who have been to combat, and the majority of your peers have been over to at least one of the two warfronts we had in the early 2000s. I just take it as God knows where you need to be and when. Still, I knew what I might be getting into by becoming involved with Nate, and he was definitely worth it, because regardless of any issues that I figured I might find that he had, he is a great man, and I knew I wanted to spend the rest of my life with him.

Nate, for the most part, is well adjusted after coming home, and you would have to really know him to see his agitations now, but years ago when we first started dating, his moods were a little more unpredictable. I believe there is a trial and error phase at the start of every relationship, so I was prepared to take him as he was and yet make a decision to drop out of the relationship if anything was too extreme about him for me to handle. I noticed he could be abrupt at times, but I was careful not to overreact to what I thought were his overreactions. He was still close enough to his deployment to be very uncomfortable passing debris on the side of the road. He had recently left an environment where a simple box or bag on the highway could very well be an explosive ready to kill or maim every occupant in the vehicle. He was still veering far away from objects like this if they were on the shoulder, and he would pay extra attention to bridges when we approached or passed under one, again, because this was a method they used over there to kill you. I can honestly say I don't think twice while driving on the highway when I pass under bridges, but if he needed to look up at the bridge, lean back, and lean forward to look at it again in order to feel better about it, I say go for it. It wasn't worth pointing it out to him and making him feel self-conscious that I was noticing these things.

There was an incident when we were driving through his hometown. I cannot even remember exactly what started the issue, but another driver was being combative, getting on our ass and abruptly swerving in the next lane, and followed it up by being in the lane next to us at a stoplight. There was a lot of cussing on Nate's part, wondering what the hell the other driver was doing, and the other driver gave Nate the finger and seemed to be using the same words Nate was, when all of a sudden Nate decided to open up his driver's side door and started to get out. I know I said I was careful not to overreact to his overreactions, but that was my end point. To that, I commenced to use some words of my own, and fortunately, Nate got back in the car, the light turned green, and we never saw that driver again, and I didn't have to post bail.

The road rage has calmed down over time with Nate. It has almost become more of joke now more than anything because, in my experience with him, instead of making issues a scolding offense or pointing out something is off, it is more beneficial to find ways to laugh at it in our case. I knew we were able to make it part of our family persona as well when we were on our way home from a vacation in South Carolina. We were having an excellent and easy drive home, but still, joking, Nate would say about cars in front of us, "Get the _ _ _ _ out of my way!" He'd edit himself for the kids, unless someone was really doing something stupid, then he would say "fuck" out loud. The kids always knew not to repeat it, and they would giggle when they heard it in this specific case.

I asked the kids, "What was your favorite part of the trip?"

Our son Taylor said the "the Blowfish game." This was the minor league team we went to watch.

Our daughter Maddy said, "The zoo!"

We had another kid in the car who is a dear family friend and now a soldier himself who was about thirteen at the time, and when I asked him what his favorite part of the trip was, he said, "Nate's road rage!" Uh oh. So his PTSD hadn't gone as unnoticed by others as we originally thought, but we still laugh at that young man's favorite part of the trip.

There are some other issues that come with Nate's PTSD that are not as easily passed by with humor, however. I remember one day we were in the house and watching something on National Geographic. We were having a conversation about it, and he walked into the kitchen, paused, and mid-conversation rushed to the sink and vomited. I ran to him, got him a washcloth, and when he collected himself, I said, surprised and concerned, "Where on earth did that come from?"

He said, "I don't know." He seemed surprised himself.

I pressed further. "Did you eat something weird?"

"No, I haven't had anything," he said.

"Are you sick? Do you have the flu?" I moved to feel his forehead.

He recoiled, on the verge of annoyance at my prying, and said, "We were watching that show on TV, and it put an image in my head of something I saw, a guy's torso in the back of a HMMWV from a blast, and it was disgusting, and then I just got sick." I remember thinking back to the show, and it wasn't about war or anything violent. I was going over this quickly in my mind so I could know what the antagonist in the program was so I could protect him in the future and make sure we didn't watch something like that again, but in all honesty, there is no way of knowing for sure what will trigger someone with war PTSD when they have so many different traumatic events accumulated in the Rolodex of their minds. There's no specific way to keep them from it when they get back home.

That afternoon when he got sick in the sink, I was genuinely surprised. During this time and many more to follow, he would get images, almost flashes, in his head of something he had seen, and his physical reaction was to get sick. This happened sometimes if he was watching something on TV that triggered it; smells sometimes initiated it, such as raw meat before I prepared it or sometimes just a random memory with what seemed like nothing in our current environment to evoke such a reaction. I realized he was dealing with more in his head than he was letting on in our conversations. These occurrences at least were a lead-in to get him to tell me some of the stories of the things he had experienced. For the first few years, I had fragments of information that helped me understand him better, and these tidbits helped guide me in how to approach the lingering issues of what he went through with what I actually knew about what he went through. The more I knew, the easier it was for me to try to help and understand what was going on when Nate had a PTSD-induced issue.

The getting sick was one thing, and a physical sign he was dealing with something, but he also had/has a mental nagging that takes more peeling back to get to, like getting to a center of an onion. He would have a random pain or cramp somewhere on his body and would start to fixate on it. He had a reoccurring pain in his side and would tell me about it. The wife and mom in me would start to analyze the basics of it first. "Maybe it's gas, or maybe you slept on it weird." He would touch it and pace around, do something else, and then bring it up again. I would try to reassure him that it was most likely nothing, and he would stay on it that something wasn't right.

When I suggested getting it checked out if he was really concerned about it, however, he would refuse.

After another pause, he would say, "Maybe it's cancer." I would think, *Oh great, I'm dealing with a hypochondriac.*

"Why would you think automatically that a cramp is cancer?" I would say, knowing he was going to dwell on the subject in his head yet refuse to do anything about it. On one hand, I think he knew it would turn out to be nothing, and on the other, I think he was afraid it would be something.

This would happen all the time with him, and finally the real concern came out. Halfway through that onion, he finally said, "I've been to combat three times, I have all my limbs, and I'm not dead. No one is that lucky. So what if this is what's going to be what finally gets me?"

There we go, now we are getting down to what the real issue is, I thought. He was dealing with his own version of survivor's remorse. So during this time and many other times, he would tell me stories of things he had to do, things that he experienced and had to see and be a part of, such as patrols and body clean-ups and seeing dead bodies in Katrina that decayed over time because the proper teams weren't in place to properly remove them. In my head, my reactions were of deep sympathy that someone I loved had to go through such life events (when just one of these events alone could throw a typical person over the edge) and also of repulsion that such horrific images are permanently etched in his memory.

To accommodate his process of being open with it, I would be sure to control my reactions. The goal was to get him to be honest about what was plaguing him and work towards getting help for it. So I listened and reacted as I knew he needed me to. I was encouraging and sympathetic. No matter how much he got off his chest during the day, however, it did not help what was happening each night.

The first few times Nate had his nightmares, it threw me off. For one thing, I was waking out of a deep sleep to someone lying next to me twitching and cussing very loudly. This can be unnerving. My experience with him and the words coming out of his mouth told me he was more than likely having a nightmare about combat. I didn't know what his reaction was going to be when I woke him up, and I knew better than to touch him to do it, so I'd carefully get out of my side of the bed and yell his name until he woke up.

"What?" he'd say, annoyed and with the same out-of-sleep confusion he woke me up with.

"You were having a nightmare, baby," I'd reply, getting back into bed.

"Oh," he would say, not denying it but a little embarrassed or sorry that I got brought into it. "I'm sorry. Go back to bed."

I would always ask him if wanted to tell me what his dream was about. Sometimes he would tell me in detail, usually if he knew there was no way that he would fall back asleep. Sometimes he would just say one word like "jawbone" or "Blue," and since he told me most of his stories, I would understand the context of what he had just dreamed of, at least. Sometimes, he just wanted to go back to sleep without getting into it. These nightmares caused daytime exhaustion, so if I thought he could go back to sleep successfully, I didn't want to press any further about whatever it was he just dreamed about.

I would say that most of his disturbing dreams are combat or Katrina related. I have enough experience with him going through this by now that I can usually tell when it is about to happen. His breathing changes when he is starting to get into it, like someone trying to suck in air through clenched teeth. Then there is some low murmuring, but I can tell he is becoming agitated. Then he starts to flat-out cuss out loud, saying things like, "Get the fuck down," or, "I'll smoke your fucking ass." His dreams are not just restricted to intense combat situations. Sometimes he'll cuss just as hard, and come to find out, he was dreaming about being back in garrison dealing with soldiers and the daily expectations of being a senior leader. Not going to lie, but when I find out non-life-threatening situations like drill sergeant duties are the subject of what he is dreaming about, I do become annoyed by being brought into it, but hey, it comes with the territory.

Often, he dreams of stressful situations in the military, such as having to repeat Ranger School (which he never had to repeat any of the phases of Ranger School but has dreams that he has to) or being a drill sergeant and having to deal with large groups of eighteen-year-olds or an issue about a field exercise. These were issues or times when he was really stressed out, and even after being out of the Army for ten years, these stresses creep back up in his sleep. He wakes up and has to remind himself that he's not there anymore and does not have to physically deal with these issues anymore. He does not have to prepare for Jumpmaster Duty or turning in insurgents, and a dead man on the roof of a car is not talking to him in New Orleans. We have learned, however, that removing yourself from the situation doesn't always make the apprehension stop.

The dreams are one issue that has not entirely lightened up over time. He made the comment to me that he never has pleasant dreams. I said, "Well, you probably do, but they just aren't the ones you remember."

He said, kind of aggressively, "No, I never have good dreams."

I know now that he might twitch during them, but he is not going to lash out at me when I wake him up. So now I just have to say his name loudly until he snaps out of it. I don't need to slide out of arms' reach. I noticed that if I don't make him fully wake up, he will often just slip right back into the same dream, so after I get him to wake up, I make him talk and maybe answer a few questions until I know he is fully awake and there's no chance of reentering the distressing dream. This makes him very annoyed by me, but hey, I've got to get back to sleep as well, so I'm not very sympathetic about him being agitated by me anymore.

Sometimes, I can tell during the day if he might have issues that night. Occasionally, watching war movies like *American Sniper* or

Black Hawk Down will elicit the nightmares. He'll watch those, and at certain parts, he'll be like, "Wow, that looks just like it over there," or, "Oh man, I've had to do that before." I'll sit next to him and think, *Yep, this may make an appearance tonight in the feature film that is Nate's dream world.* Sometimes, he'll watch something non-military but maybe gory, and that will cause it, too. News stories have caused the nightmares. We often fall asleep with the TV on in the room, and depending on what the big news stories are, they could bring a nightmare on, I think just from him hearing it subconsciously as he is falling asleep. We watched a story where the 82nd Airborne Division was on a rapid deployment to the Middle East recently, and he was like, "Funny, I think I just wrote a book about this exact thing." He was referring to his first book, *Division: Life on Ardennes Street*, and lo and behold, he had a few nights in a row where he was cussing under his breath. I lay there and predict from what he is saying whether it is going to escalate or not, as I mentioned. I have to assess and make a decision on how bad I think the dream might be, because it's difficult for him to finally get to sleep in the first place, and sometimes if I think he will get out of the bad part on his own, I'll just leave him alone. Doesn't help my sleep situation much, but even though he is asleep, he's not always actually getting rest, if that makes sense.

Nate's nightmares were something he had right off the bat in our relationship. At the time we got together, he had already been to combat twice, and sure enough, after a couple months of marriage, we were at a new duty station and were gearing up for his third combat deployment. During this time, he had a lot of responsibility getting the unit ready for mobilization. He wasn't sleeping very much, but when he did, it was like he would go straight to a nightmare. The situation was probably at its worst during this time. He wasn't getting quality rest, he was stressed out at work, and this caused him to be more irritable.

I remember one situation while I was working on my MBA. I lost a nine-page paper just hours before it was due. My computer just up and crashed, and there was no getting it back. He was completely unsympathetic and told me to just write it again. I had a breakdown and cried at the loss of what I thought was a really great paper, and then I was furious with him for being so callous about it. He tried to pretend to care after he saw my reaction and even called his S-6 (communications) sergeant, and he agreed there was nothing I could do to recover it. My computer had simply died, and I wasn't smart enough to back the paper up on another source, purely my issue and my fault. Still, it hurt that he really was so disinterested in my current problem.

I understood that Nate was stressed out about something I couldn't truly empathize with. For him, he knew how horrible the place was that he was going to. He had to deal with knowing he was going back to the worst place on earth, and since he was Torch Party (the very first people from a unit to hit ground on deployment to ensure the rest of the unit arrives in country smoothly), he knew he had a lot to do and would be there longer than the standard year. While he was gone, of course, I was on pins and needles. The news did not help put me at ease at all. They would name places I knew he was at and show IED attack aftermath, and my mind would go in a million directions, wondering: *What he's doing now? Is he okay? When will he call again?* One such instance was right around Christmas the year he was deployed. I was staying at my parents' house and walking into the living room when I heard the name of a shrine that I knew Nate had mentioned before in random conversation. I remember sitting there staring at the TV feeling sick to my stomach, hearing the news repeat the horrid details and begging Nate in my mind to call soon.

He only called every other week and only for a short time, but we e-mailed every day, which didn't feel the same. I looked forward to his calls so much, just to hear his voice, but was irritated that for the first five minutes of every call, I had to listen to him cussing about the Ugandans taking up all the phone time. "These guys must be really fucking popular in fucking Uganda, let me tell you," he would say. I'd roll my eyes and get to whatever needed to be discussed because I knew we didn't have long to talk. He had to get back to the TOC (Tactical Operations Center). I think he thought if he left the TOC for too long that he was jinxing his guys into something bad happening, and he felt that they were safer somehow if he specifically was the one monitoring their movements. I knew he rarely left it, and the men above and below him mentioned when they were back home how long and hard he worked in there. We attended a Military Ball after he was home for a few months, and soldiers of all ranks came up to me, shook my hand, and gave testimonials about how great Nate did over there and how much they could count on him.

I knew in my heart at home that he would come back home and intact, but I had to keep myself busy, so I did what I'm sure many military spouses do. I worked out and read a lot. I slept on his side of the bed in his T-shirts. I tried to avoid the news, and then with morbid curiosity, I'd turn it on and instantly regret it and then change the channel again. I sent care packages on the first of the month to start with. I'd send a carton of Marlboro Reds and a log (containing five cans) of Copenhagen. Toward mid-deployment, he asked sometime around the twentieth of the month, "Baby, where's my care package at?"

I said, "I send those on the first of the month." Trust me, I knew when it was time to send it; I dreaded it. The lines at post offices around military installations at wartime were miserable. It didn't matter which one you went to.

"Well, I'm out of tobacco, so please send one today. And send two cartons and two logs of chew," he ordered.

I thought, *Okay . . . so he's chain smoking now, I take it.* So I started to send two of each instead of one, and by the end of the deployment, he was asking for them before the first of the month again. This started to make me think about what he was going to be like when he got home. How bad was his smoking now? Was he going to have health issues from it? I knew his agitation level was high, but was he going to take it out on me? Would he still even be funny and loving? I couldn't help but have some of these thoughts and questions cross my mind, knowing that this kind of experience he was going through could really change a person and not always for the better.

While he was gone, I got the word from my National Guard unit that they finally found a slot for me in the Environmental Science School I had been waiting for. *Great!* I thought, then I saw the report date on my orders, and I was to be there the week before Nate got home. It was a nine-week course. My heart sank, and he just so happened to call me that night. I told him about it and couldn't help but cry at the poor timing. He said, "Hey, it's fine. You've really been wanting that school, and we've already gone this long. What's a couple more months?"

"You're right. I just miss you," I said. All the other spouses saw their soldier at some point during the deployment, but I never saw Nate because he refused to take mid-tour leave. He said from experience that with two weeks of leave, it would take him the whole first week just to get to the point where he could relax, and the second week he'd be all amped up again knowing he needed to go back, so there was no point.

So he replied to the issue of my schooling with, "I miss you, too, but don't miss out on this just because of the timing of it." My heart warmed up at the realization that he was still considerate and loving, and his situation over there didn't change that.

So I left for Texas, and a week later, he came home to an empty apartment, a full ice cube tray, and a bottle of his favorite scotch on the counter with a note from me. I had also washed all of his civilian clothes because after not being worn for a year, except for the T-shirts I was wearing to bed, they all smelled stale, and I didn't want him to be disappointed by that. These are things you don't think about generally because it's not normal to go a year without wearing your own clothes. I felt bad because a friend of ours had to pick him up from the homecoming on post. Usually, the spouses are there ready to receive their soldier with hugs and kisses. Instead, our friend helped him with his bags and drove him to our apartment. I had dropped off our door key to him before I left because I remembered that Nate didn't have one with him. That would have sucked finally coming home after being gone all that time and realizing you couldn't get in. We couldn't just leave his truck up at his unit because technically the soldier coming home isn't allowed to drive for a week because they have to acclimate to stateside life again. It's probably a good idea to settle in first.

So Nate was deployed for thirteen months when all was said and done for his final combat deployment. I had two months of school left to go when he got back, and finally after fifteen long months, we were able to be together again. He was more or less the same, still my funny and loving husband. He was agitated often, just as he was before, and there were now non-combat stresses he had to deal with, such as us building a home in Ohio while we lived in Kansas and starting the retirement process, all events in life that will stress out any person. But coming out of a deployment, and not truly decompressing yet, he was still kind of on edge and often got short with people quickly.

I remember we were watching the news, and the NFL championship game hosted at the Superdome in New Orleans was the big topic. The coverage showed footage of inside the Superdome and interviews with people of New Orleans outside, mostly talking about the Saints' excellent year and the hardships of surviving Hurricane Katrina. Nate freaked out. "They can't have people in there!"

"People can't go in where? What are you talking about?" I said. I was legitimately surprised by his outburst.

"In the Superdome! Don't you know what went on in there? There were dirty diapers everywhere in the stands, garbage and waste everywhere, bodies in one of the halls. Little girls were getting raped in the bathroom. There was a guy floating in the parking garage so long his face peeled off of his head. They can't let people back in there!" he yelled.

"Well," I said, seeing he was genuinely upset and being careful of my words, "I'm sure they've cleaned it up since then. That was four years ago, baby."

"They should have torn it down the second they got everyone out of there." He left the room and still does not want to watch games that are hosted there. Sure enough, that night he had a very intense nightmare. He was cussing and breathing harder than I had ever experienced with him before, and this time, I actually had to shake him to wake him up because he was not answering when I yelled his name. He woke up physically upset; I thought he might get sick, and I was shaken at how distraught he was.

"You were having a nightmare," I said.

"I know. Tell me about it," he said, finally steadying himself.

"What was going on in it? You were yelling some really crazy stuff."

"It was the Superdome. But there were no lights, and it almost felt like a zombie movie. The dead were waking up and coming after us, and we couldn't find a way out. It was horrible."

Wow! Dream or not, that is some crazy shit to have to deal with. When the military spouses get together, they like to talk about resources and tell each other to call them if you ever need anything, the "you are not alone" jargon, but at night laying there with your husband breathing heavy and physically upset, you are alone. It was at this juncture that I suggested maybe seeing a counselor. There was a stigma up to this point in the military that you shouldn't go to counseling for PTSD because then it's a part of your medical records. This is a myth, by the way. It is not looked at as weakness that you identified that you needed to speak to someone, and you will not be passed for promotion or discriminated against for it. For Nate, he knew he had completed his final deployment, and he was starting the retirement process, so he figured what did he have to lose either way? He started to see a counselor on post, and it was a great help and a step in the right direction.

All these years later, Nate still sees a counselor regularly, and often they don't even talk about the wars or combat or even his time in the military but the everyday issues he encounters. For career soldiers, even those who only spent a few years in, I'm sure, there are expectations of the actions of those around you. There is the expectation of promptness, order, and decisiveness of people you deal with, and most civilians do not operate this way. Nate will lose his patience with the kids and his friends sometimes. I'm former military, and I've even had to tell him, "I'm not one of your soldiers. Don't talk to me like that. Relax." Old habits die hard.

His patience is better than when he was active duty but still is not as strong as most civilians. He loses his patience quick when technology is not working in the way he thinks it should. Before losing his cool, he'll usually sic me on it to troubleshoot the issue. He gets extremely agitated when I vacuum. The noise bothers him, and I know it's not pleasant, but most people can deal with it knowing it needs done. I have to hear, "Hurry up with that!" any time I do it when he is home, so I strategically try to do it when he is out, which, with him being retired, is not exactly consistent.

There are also still other lingering effects from everything Nate has experienced. Some of these have leaked into his personal relationships. I am Nate's third wife. This is common for combat arms veterans to have had a few wives; it's a rough life to follow. He has had freak-out moments when he admitted to me later that it crossed his mind, *Uh oh, when is this one going to leave me?* We are solid, though, and by this point, he should be sure that I am not going anywhere. He is quick to let go of people who create toxic relationships, such as friends and family who do not treat him with respect. This is good, because you shouldn't be anyone's doormat, yet he also has a fear of abandonment from those who are close to him. This gets difficult sometimes, because often those close to him have no idea what he has been through or they downplay it because they just don't get it and never will. For Nate, I think he's often lonely even when surrounded by people due to the typical people in our circle not having a frame of reference close to his. So often he will be itching to go out and see friends, and then once there, he says, "Are you ready to leave?"

This is me laying out some of the key elements that as a wife of a veteran with PTSD I've personally dealt with. I know this all seems like a hot mess seeing it compressed in this way, but it really isn't. Trust me, Nate does not have more issues than a lot of civilians we know; it's just different for him because we know where the issues stem from and he has solid reasons for them. I've never wavered in my feelings for him, but deciding early that, hell or high water, I was going to stick it out with him means a life of extreme patience and unconditional love.

Nate and I have been together for almost fourteen years now, and I finally have the majority of his stories and experiences laid out in a comprehensive manner, yet I feel like I am still learning about him every day. I feel more prepared than ever to help us move forward with our life together. As time has marched on, it has gotten better and better with every passing day. Even with all the counseling on Nate's part, however, and the understanding I have developed on my part, I have no expectation of the bad dreams stopping. I know in the coming nights I will have to speak out in the middle of the night and say, "Nate, wake up! You are having another nightmare."

Nate and I on our wedding day December 7, 2007

Nate and I ten years after his retirement from the Army. Current day.

CHAPTER 7

COUNSELING AFTER RETIREMENT

After thirteen months in Iraq, without any days off, I was quite on edge when I got home, as I was before. I didn't even take mid-tour leave, primarily for two reasons: one, by the time I got home and got back on the timeline with everyone else, it would be time to go back to the worse place on earth, and two, I was also saving up my leave for what the military calls terminal leave, due to me planning on retiring when we got back. The only two days I wasn't working in the tactical operation center of our battalion was when I had the swine flu, or H1N1. It got to the point that I simply did not leave the TOC, only to sleep for a few hours, and then I was back in there. Even my buddy who was Bravo Company's First Sergeant tried several times to get me to go to chow with him, but I would always refuse to leave. I had the paranoid mentality that the second I would leave the operations shop, somebody would get hit by the enemy out in sector. So, therefore, I would have one of my soldiers bring me a to-go plate of food.

I ended up getting that damn H1N1 flu because it was going around big time in 2009, and soldiers were bringing it back with them from the States when they would go home on their mid-tour leave. I remember how I got it, too. A soldier had a to-go plate of chow for dinner one evening, and I ate the rest of his for him instead of getting my own plate. We didn't care; we were all infantry guys anyway. That was our mentality. Come to find out, the damn kid had that flu, and I got it from eating off his plate. It was some bad shit, too. I remember the Command Sergeant Major walking in the TOC, and I had my head down because I was so fucking hot. He asked me what was wrong, and I told him I was sick. He told me to get out of the TOC and to go back to my trailer to lay down. He said not to come back until I felt better.

I said, "Roger that, Sergeant Major." My throat was so fucking sore, too, that I went straight to the latrine trailer and looked in the mirror. I opened my mouth and had white bags of puss in the back of my throat. I said to myself, "What the fuck?" I went to my trailer and turned off the air conditioning because I was freezing by this time. It was like July in Iraq. So you're talking it was about one hundred twenty degrees outside, too. I remember even putting on a sweatshirt and getting all bundled up with my wooby and going straight to sleep. I literally slept for two days straight. I'm not shitting you. When I finally woke up, I felt good again. I shaved, showered, put on a clean uniform, and went back to work in the TOC. That was some wicked shit. I don't think I've ever been sick since. Let me knock on some wood really quick.

When I got back from Iraq, my wife was away at a school in Fort Sam Houston, Texas. So, after our brigade was complete with our mandatory two-week recovery time on Fort Riley, I flew down to visit her on a four-day weekend. I hadn't seen her in almost fourteen months. I remember getting off the plane, still in my uniform, and she came running across the terminal to hug and kiss me. I remember that first night as we were walking back from the strip in San Antonio, I started breaking down into tears. She asked what was wrong, and I couldn't explain what it was. I knew at that point that something was wrong with me.

A couple of weeks later, when she was back home, she immediately discovered that I was having nightmares every single night, and she was constantly waking me up from them. "Honey, I think it's time you go get some help," she'd said to me. I was reluctant to, because I was afraid to be labeled as crazy. Like I explained in *Division*, you didn't dare go to the post mental health facility unless you wanted to lose your duty position, especially back in the day. However, she talked me into it, and her convincing factor was that I was retiring in eleven months anyway. I said okay. She actually went with me to that first appointment, where I was diagnosed with having Post-Traumatic Stress Disorder within forty-five minutes of being evaluated by the psychiatrist, as I stated in the beginning of this book.

After the evaluation, I went ahead and made my first appointment with him for the following week. My wife was able, and he even encouraged me to bring her, in order to get her experiences with me, which basically was having bad dreams and a little road rage, as she just described during her chapter she wrote. When we got to our first appointment, I sat with my back towards the wall on the far side of his office, facing the door. My wife sat in the other chair. It was somewhat of a dark setting, with the room only lit up with a small lamp that he had in the corner. The chairs were leather and pretty comfortable to sit in. It was your typical setting for a counseling session with a psychiatrist, like you see in the movies.

"So, tell me anything you wish, Nathan," he said to me.

I started talking to him about my nightmares I was having quite regularly. I didn't waste any time, especially since I didn't even want to be there. As a matter of fact, I was having anxiety just thinking about going, and it started the night before. I told him about the guy from my first OIF deployment that we picked up all over the highway. Then I told him about Katrina with "Blue," "Chester the I-10 Infester," and of course "Bobby Boucher." After that, I told him about my last deployment we had just got back from and just simply the eeriness of being back over there, along with the long hours and tensions between everyone. I know some may think, *Well, you were in Operations the whole year. You shouldn't have any stresses from that experience.* Well, it was just that. When you're in the TOC eighteen or nineteen hours a day for three hundred sixty-five days straight, tensions will rise, like I explained in the previous chapter.

He then asked my wife for her input, and she began to explain to him her experiences with me over the past three years we had been together. She pretty much covered down on everything she wrote about in the previous chapter, so I won't repeat everything she has already mentioned. He then asked her the magic question: "Do you feel threatened or harmed when you're with Nathan?" Of course, she said no, that she knew how to handle my nightmares and "rage" episodes.

We had spent at least two hours with him that first counseling session. He asked me if I would be willing to write my stories out and perhaps draw a picture of each. He explained that it was cognitive behavioral therapy and that it was proven to be very effective. I told him sure, I would give it a try. He then handed me a box of colored pencils and told me to bring at least one back the following week when I was to visit him again. I brought him back three or four. One thing I have generally been pretty decent at my whole life is drawing.

When I came back the following week, I sat in the same seat, and so did my wife. He had me read to him each story and then show him my pictures I drew. "I must say that I am impressed with your work," he said to me.

"Thanks, Doc," I replied to him. He was a cool guy, with a pretty good personality. In other words, he wasn't a "stiff" like you might expect most of your older, experienced psychiatrists to be. I actually was feeling pretty comfortable going to his counseling sessions every week. I pretty much went to him weekly until I signed out on terminal leave and retired. Those original writings and pictures are displayed in my few pics at the end of this chapter.

After a few more months, I signed out on terminal leave and drove out of not only Fort Riley, but the Army as a whole. Twenty years of my life was spent in one of the best organizations on the planet. I am so proud to have served this great nation, and I wouldn't change anything I did, because even some bad things that I may have done as a younger soldier taught me to be more of a responsible adult. It also taught me life lessons in this world. Like *Forrest Gump* said one time, "And just like that, my time in the United States Army was over."

After I was established in our new home we had built in northwest Ohio, I continued to seek counseling. So I began with a behavioral counseling center in a nearby city, about ten miles away. I was *not* comfortable with this place at all. There were some very disturbed individuals. A couple of them wore helmets and talked to themselves. I told my wife, "Honey, I don't think I belong here." She suggested that we simply get up and leave. I told her that I would stick it out and at least meet the counselor.

The counselor was a middle-aged woman who was a certified social worker for the State of Ohio. I was completely honest with her, with the fact that it was very disturbing for me sitting out in that waiting room and being around those people. She said she completely understood and said to me, "Oh, yeah, we have some interesting characters that come in and out of here." She had also confessed to me that she was not necessarily up to speed with dealing with individuals with Post-Traumatic Stress Disorder, especially within the military. I told her I completely understood as well. So we started out being very honest with one another that first session together.

The next session a couple of weeks later went a little smoother. She had done some research and was more up to speed on counseling a soldier with PTSD. I told her that I had appreciated her efforts. She was a nice lady, with concern about military that I could tell. However, as soon as my terminal leave was up and I was officially retired from the Army, I immediately made my first appointment with the nearest VA. You see, I could not go to the VA before, because technically, I was still on active duty when we first got to Ohio.

I remember trying to get a copy of my records from the behavioral place, but they would not release them to me. Of course, I got extremely pissed off, and of course, I let them know about it.

The lady in the administrative section holding all the records was not cooperative or pleasant, and I let her know how I felt about it. Anyway, I went ahead and made my first appointment at the VA.

When I first got there, I checked in with the Silver Clinic, which is the mental health counseling section of the establishment. For the first time, I met my counselor, whom I continue to see to this day—ten years later. She is awesome and has become somebody I can definitely trust. We also have become good friends to this day as well. She always tells me that I'm one of her best patients because I'm calm and polite. I guess she gets some real assholes in there weekly, if not daily. She also runs several group counseling sessions weekly as well.

The first time I met her, we did an introductory session in her office. I felt comfortable with her right off the bat. Again, I was quite nervous and had plenty of anxiety from the night before, all the way until I got to her office that first day. Hell, I didn't know what to expect because I was going to the VA, for Christ's sake, and the waiting rooms in that place can be very hectic. I still get anxiety to this day when I go there for counseling. I don't even sit down. Instead, I stand in one spot and grab a magazine. I usually keep my face in it the whole time I wait for her to come out and get me. I choose to not look around or interact with any of the other veterans because, again, there are some real unstable individuals that go to the VA.

Anyway, getting back to our first session together. The first thing she asked me was if I had any previous counseling, and I told her about my sessions at Fort Riley and the few sessions I attended at the behavioral center. She said, "Oh man, you went to there? Wow, how did you handle that?"

I said, "Not so good."

She asked me if they gave me my records so that she could get a copy for her files. I told her they refused to give them to me, and she said she would request them. It made sense to me coming from one medical center directly to another. They never did give them to her, either. Oh well. That place sucked ass completely.

She asked me a list of questions from a mandatory form that she had to fill out in order to begin my records. It was pretty much all digital. She began asking me what my Military Occupational Skill (job in the Army) was. She asked my rank and how many years I had spent in the Army. She then went into combat deployments and asked about locations, dates I was over there, and my duty assignments for each. We then got into my nightmares and my road rage incidences. She completely understood and had heard it all many times before. I definitely was with a counselor that was experienced with veterans, in particular, Global War on Terrorism veterans. At that time, she was the primary counselor for Afghanistan and Iraq veterans. She also ran a group session weekly with these same veterans as well. She had asked me if I would be interested in signing up to attend them. "If you can't make every week, it's not a big deal. I understand that not everyone can make it."

"Will I get penalized by the VA if I miss any sessions?"

"No, not at all," she assured me.

"I have heard stories of other veterans that were kicked out of the VA system for missing one scheduled appointment."

"Not for missing any of my sessions," she assured me. I told her I would be interested in trying out the group sessions. She then signed me up, and the next week, I was in the first group.

At the beginning of the session, she introduced me to the rest of the group and had me say a few words to them of my veteran status. I kept it short and just said my name and what rank I was and how long I had spent in the Army. I then went into how many deployments I had and what years. She then had each veteran introduce themselves to me, and we went around the table. It was pretty standard every time a new veteran joined the group.

There were about a dozen of us, mostly marines, a couple of soldiers, a couple of airman, and I do not believe we had anybody from the Navy in there. The sessions were great, without any specific format, and that is what made them so great. We all would simply go around the table and tell whatever was on our minds for that week. It was usually nothing to do with the war but everyday complications we were having in civilian life, everything from driving on the roads or highways, asshole drivers, incidences at restaurants, problems at home, with kids, with spouses, etc., etc. It was a real valuable hour we would spend talking to one another.

The ranks ranged from private first class to senior noncommissioned officers. Hell, we even had a field grade officer in there with us. Before our meetings, we would all sit together out in the waiting room. We all became close and had a strong comradery with one another. We had one veteran that still attends to this day; I mean, we all do, pretty much, except for one or two that moved too far away eventually. He was a double amputee below the waist and was in a wheelchair. He was a sergeant in the 101st Airborne. I never asked him, because I didn't have to, due to him having the stickers on the back of his wheelchair. He had gotten hit with an IED in Iraq in 2006. Not only was he in a wheelchair, but he had traumatic brain injury, along with obviously PTSD as well. His traumatic brain injury was severe, so severe that he forgot how to read and write.

It was sad, especially when I first started going to the group sessions. That was one of two things we all had in common: one, we were all Afghanistan and/or Iraq veterans, and two, we were all clinically diagnosed with PTSD. Going back to the young Sergeant in the wheelchair, he was cool, with a great sense of humor. So it made me feel better and more comfortable to be around him. He would always purposely bump his wheelchair in or going out of the door, and then he would say, "Ouch—my leg!" We would all start laughing.

One time he did it, and we had some representative or evaluator from our higher headquarters VA come down. She was uptight and didn't find him to be funny when he did it in front of her. She even said something to him like, "That's not funny."

He responded with, "It is for me."

I thought to myself, *What's her problem?* I can't believe she said that to him. If that's how he deals with being handicapped for the rest of his life, with a little humor, then fuck her. That was a very interesting session, so I'll tell you a little more about it.

She came down that afternoon to evaluate our session, and she would take it back to the actual VA hospital that our clinic fell under. Like I said, she was not a real pleasant person. She was arrogant and not very tolerant at all. She actually made our entire group very anxious and uncomfortable. I told a story about some kid driving through my yard and putting ruts in my newly planted grass out in front of my new house. I said the next night I sat in my living room with my AR-15 rifle, and if they did it again, I was going to go out and shoot out their tires. Would I really do it? I'm not sure at that time in my life. I was quite intolerant when somebody fucked with my family or my property. The guys in the group started laughing when I told them that little story about my week. She immediately began to chastise me in front of the group.

"Wait a minute. That is not funny at all. Do you really believe that going to jail is worth it over your grass getting messed up?" she sarcastically asked.

"Yes, I do. You obviously do not equate to this group or our mentalities, do you?" I turned the sarcasm back on her and started "sharp-shooting" her ass in front of the group. I'm not a very confrontational person, especially these days, but she obviously did not have a clue how to talk to people, especially in a setting such as the one we were in. We all felt as if she was talking down to us like we were a bunch of nobodies. You could tell the actual counselor wasn't having her at all.

One of the guys in the group looked at her and said, "Let me tell you about life, young lady. I was an MP and am also a retired police officer, so don't come in here talking to us as if we don't know anything about responsibility or life." She got up and left the room, never to be seen in our VA clinic again. At least not in our group sessions anymore. I remember feeling bad for our counselor because

I'm sure that lady's report wasn't very good when she got back up to the other VA hospital.

Speaking of making our group upset, we had a new member join one time about a year later. He had a service dog with him. It was a cute little dog and well behaved, as expected. Anyway, he was telling us that earlier, before they got to the VA, the dog didn't do something he said. He said when he got home that evening, he was going to take the dog out back of his house and shoot it and kill it. We all got really quiet at that particular point of the session. He then tried to change the subject on us. Another member of the group cut him off and said, "Wait, let's go back to what you said about your dog."

He replied, "I said when I get home tonight, I'm going to kill the fucking thing. Why, you got a fucking problem with that?"

"Actually, yes, I do, you fucking piece of shit!" They went back and forth for about thirty seconds, and then the counselor told the guy with the dog to get up and leave the room. He was never to be seen by us again. He was immediately dismissed and removed from our group. You cannot be in the group if you are going to cause animosity among the other veterans. You definitely cannot be disrespectful to one another and call each other names, like this asshole did to my buddy. We were all about to jump on his ass, and I think the counselor knew it, too. That's why she had to get rid of his sorry ass. That definitely was somebody that thought he was "owed" something from the VA. That was my biggest problem. There were certain people in the VA facilities that thought they were owed something and all they could do was bitch all the time. It used to, and still does, piss me off to this day when I go in there. I mean, the VA has always treated me good, at least for the last ten years I've been going. Oh well, what are you going to do? You can't please everybody, right?

About two or three years into our group sessions, they began structuring the format and dictating to our counselor on how she was to run each one. It was starting to become a pain in the ass to go, because it was so structured and all. We even started receiving homework assignments and had to bring them in the following week. It was being structured to be a "progressive style" of group counseling, and it was driving us nuts. Some of the guys in the group even stopped showing up, and eventually the VA disbanded the group all together. It was so effective before when we all could go in there weekly and get off our chests the difficulties we were having with our lives. We were actually receiving therapy during those sessions. Then, when the VA started dictating to our counselor how she was to run each group, it truly became ineffective for all of us.

Anyway, so the VA got rid of our group, but we would all individually see our counselor for at least an hour per session. I was, and still do, regularly go on an average of twice a month. For a while there, the VA created a new group that was conducted by another counselor. Actually, she wasn't much of a counselor because she too was so formatted "by the book." I and a couple of the others from the original group stopped going to her all together. Too easy, right?

When I go in for my one-on-one sessions with her today, we discuss issues I have with friends and family, problems with the American Legion I belong to or some of the students I have when I teach at the school, etc. From time to time, she will ask me about what some of my stresses in the 82nd Airborne Division were during my nine years I was there. You've heard a lot of those stories in *Division*, but one of the biggest stresses I had was my last three years I was there.

During my last three years, every single time we had a jump, I was selected to be a Primary Jumpmaster. Not that I couldn't handle it. Actually, I was very good at it and had it down to a science. I'm not bullshitting you, I could rattle off the entire Sustained Airborne Training, or Pre-jump, like it was nothing. That is about seven pages of a memorized format that had to be given to the jumpers generally word for word.

If I wasn't doing Jumpmaster duties in the air, I was selected to the Primary DZSO or Drop Zone Safety Officer on the ground for another unit jumping. DZSO has a major responsibility as well, such as having an entire ground crew on the drop zone. I was responsible to ensure we had a rescue crew ready to retrieve jumpers that were in the trees, which happened from time to time, or simply any injured paratrooper on the ground after their jump. We had to have a complete medical crew on standby with us on the drop zone, along with two of us monitoring the wind speeds on the ground.

The Assistant DZSO and I would each have a wind-speed indicator, which was a little handheld device that you would hold up in the air and then the knots or speed of the wind would read on it. I would then report it to the pilot of the lead aircraft coming into the drop zone from above, usually at about eight hundred feet above ground level. I would get on my radio, which would be set to the pilot's frequency, and the conversation would go something like this:

"Tin Can 6, this is Sicily Drop Zone, over."

"Sicily, this is Tin Can 6, I read you loud and clear, over."

"Roger, wind speed is six knots, you are clear to drop, over."

"Roger, Sicily, I read you that we are clear to drop, over."

It was kind of funny, because they would speak to you in the same polite voice that any pilot does when you fly on any civilian airline. If the winds were thirteen knots or higher the mission would become a "No-Drop."

Not only would I call and verbally tell the pilot and get confirmation from him or her, but I would have to tell my crew to turn off each of the signal lights for the code letter on the lead edge of the drop zone. I would also be located at the lead edge, as well, with the medics. That would be the visual signal for them not to jump as well. During the daylight hours, the code letter would be VS-17 bright orange panels. Each drop zone on Fort Bragg would have their own code letter. However, I never got so lucky as to have thirteen knot winds and have a jump cancelled for it. Nope, I would be stuck out there the whole time until I linked up with the Airborne Commander on the ground after all of the chalks landed and he received each company's report of personnel, equipment accountability, and any injuries. Once he or she would give me the report, I was clear to police up the entire detail and leave the drop zone.

I would send the entire crew back to our battalion, but I would have to go directly back to Pope Air Force Base and give them a briefing and also turn in their radios that they would issue me. DZSO duties were under the Air Force jurisdiction. However, if you fucked up and gave a bad wind reading by mistake, for example, your ass would be fired, and depending on if anyone got hurt, you would probably receive punishment under the Uniformed Code of Military Justice. So you had your stresses on this duty, as you do in the air as well.

One evening after DZSO duty, I got home around 0300. Man, it was a late night, and I was so fucking tired but excited as well. I was excited to see my wife and two kids, who had been on vacation for the past couple of weeks, back home with her family. When I got home from Pope Air Force Base, the house was still empty. So I called her cell phone to ask where they were at. I figured they stopped and got a hotel or something on the long ride home. When I asked her, she got really quiet all of a sudden. "What is wrong?" I asked her.

"I filed for divorce, and I'm not coming back," she told me. Like Forrest Gump used to say, 'That's all I have to say about that."

Anyhow, my name is Nate Aguinaga. I am a retired Infantryman from the U.S. Army who has been diagnosed with Post-Traumatic Stress Disorder since 2009 while on active duty. I wouldn't change *any* experience or event during my time in the military, primarily because I love this country too much to worry about me having trouble sleeping throughout the nights. Who cares, right? It has all been very much worth it, and I would do again, and again . . . After all, we all can sleep well at night because we are in the United States of America.

Honestly, I did not want to write this book. When you write these stories down, you have to take yourself back into the experience that you are writing about. It is and was very difficult for me to do, but I did it. My daughter Madyson and my wife Jessica actually convinced me to write this, so I did. Writing this took more courage than anything I ever did in my twenty years in the Army. "Thank you, God, for me being alive."

I also had another nightmare last night, and I don't truly remember what exactly it was about, but my wife woke me up again. I'm sure it was about me failing to make a military timeline or something to that effect. Again, my biggest fear in my twenty years of military service wasn't combat, jumping out of airplanes, or leaving my family. My biggest fear was failure of my duties—period. I couldn't go back to sleep afterwards. I have been up since two forty-five this morning. It's all good. I think I'll make a pot a coffee and start my day.

Iraq. Plotting our next route for the next location we were ordered to move to. The messed-up part is that I let the platoon leader borrow my new Garmin that I just bought before the deployment because he forgot his back at the FOB. He had forgotten mine and left it on the hood of this vehicle when we pulled out to move to the next location. Bye-bye, brand new Garmin and $120 . . . Damn platoon leader. He used to piss me off often, but what are you going to do? I still loved the bastard and took care of him . . .

"Knock and talks" in Latifiyah, as described. Notice the twelve-gauge shotgun being carried for front door key purposes if need be. Sometimes it was needed for close encounters for other reasons . . . He was also carrying an M-4 Carbine as his primary, which you can't see in this particular picture. He was my 1st Squad Leader. We did not play around in this environment. Everybody must go home.

Me passing out candy to some of the kids in Latifiyah as we were patrolling through the streets daily.

Me and my weapons squad leader with a father and his son who used to give us help from time to time. Great people and proud farmers. We had a tight rapport with these families in our sectors of responsibility.

Dismounted patrol into a compound. We were trying to find out who the hell was mortaring our base every night, as I explained in the first chapter.

Same compound. I'll be damned. We caught these dudes with a complete mortar weapon system and over a dozen mortar rounds. They were going back to FOB Saint Michael with us that day. Way too easy.

Drill Sergeant "Augi" 2000-2002 Fort Jackson, South Carolina.

The following write ups and drawings are my originals from eleven years ago when I started Cognitive Behavioral Therapy while at my last duty station, as mentioned in the book earlier.

Hurricane Katrina Aftermath
Superdome
September, 2005

One day my unit was assigned to move over and conduct rescue operations at the Superdome. We were told that all we were going to find was a lot of trash and perhaps some dead bodies here and there, but probably not any survivors. However, there were stories of people still trying to get to the Superdome area because of food and water. This was the area where over a hundred buses lined up to evacuate the majority of New Orleans two weeks prior, on day two after the hurricane.

As we approached the outer corridor of the stadium, the stench was starting to become overwhelming, not to mention, the temperature was still almost 100 degrees. As far as the eye could see, there were piles upon piles of trash, boxes after boxes of Meals Ready to Eat (MRE)s, and shopping carts filled with household items. People were grabbing shopping carts from local stores and packing whatever they could from their homes before making their way across the city to the Superdome to be evacuated.

We entered the parking garage from the top level and moved our way down as far as we could go to the flooded water area which was all the way up to the third level or so. As we reached the lowest level we could get to, we noticed a body floating face down. The area was completely dark so we had to use the flash lights that were mounted to the barrels of our rifles in order to see anything. The body was totally disgusting, floating with arms and legs spread, and the most distinct feature from him was the decaying flesh that was attached but was coming apart from his face and arms. This sight or smell, I will never forget. He had a water bottle lodged perfectly in his back pocket – we nicknamed him "The Waterboy".

HURRICAN KATRINA AFTERMATH
9th Ward District, New Orleans
September, 2005
Nathan J. Aguinaga

As my unit was deployed to Hurricane Katrina, we drove around, not only through the flooded neighborhoods, but all around other parts of the city of New Orleans as well. Just outside the Naval Reserve Complex, approximately a half of mile down the road, we had noticed right away that there was a body wrapped in a white sheet in a parking lot, up against the stone wall that separated city from the river water-way. Above the body was a spray-painted message that said, "Fuck You Katrina", with an arrow that was pointed down towards the body. As the days went by, just the same as all other corpses that were lying randomly throughout the city, this body was still lying next to this wall without any attention given by FEMA or whatever city emergency crew that was around. About two weeks after the hurricane, we drove by the body to see if it was still lying there, and noticed that there were two neat, organized, piles of trash on both sides of the corpse. It was one of the most shocking scenes of our 30 day deployment to the city. We did not give this particular body a fictitious name, but it is one of the strongest images burned into my mind.

E.O.D. EXLOSION INCIDENT ON ASR JACKSON
MAHMUDIYAH, IRAQ—FEB 2004
Nathan J. Aguinaga

It was around 1730 one particular evening in Mahmudiyah, Iraq. My platoon was heading back to the FOB after a relatively easy-going day conducting "Knock and Talks" throughout neighborhoods in the Lutafiyah area. As we were traveling North on ASR Jackson, we received a radio call to respond to a recent IED and that there was a death of a US Soldier involved as well. We made it to the scene relatively quickly, and secured both sides of the highway, blocking off traffic from entering. Another Platoon from our FOB arrived within minutes after we did with additional Medical personnel. They began picking up pieces of this Staff Sergeant that was blown all over the median from this IED explosion. Members from his EOD crew were telling me that he had walked up to clear the first IED that had been detonated and destroyed. When he arrived to the small crater it had left, a secondary IED blew up next to him, literally blowing him all over the place. One of my Soldiers walked up to me and tried to hand me a piece of this SSG's jaw. I told him to get it out my face, to take it over to the Medics. As I turned to look towards the Humvee that had this Soldier's body parts in the cargo portion, I saw a Soldier pick up his torso and threw it in the back of the vehicle, like it was a bale of hay. The torso had no head arms or legs attached. A local fire department arrived and began spraying off the road on both sides. When I asked why they were spraying the road, the other EOD Soldiers told me it was because we couldn't leave the smallest pieces of this Soldier on the road. Our Chain of Command instructed that we were not to leave until the fire department had sprayed both sides of the highway, thoroughly. We complied and secured the sight until they were finished. We finally returned to the FOB on or about 2130. At the time it bothered me and my Soldiers, but it is an event that wasn't forgotten for the remaining time in Theater and after we got back to Ft. Bragg. The image is imbedded in my head, and I often have nightmares of this particular scene.

HURRICAN KATRINA AFTERMATH
9th Ward District, New Orleans
September, 2005
Nathan J. Aguinaga

In late August of 2005, I was alerted to report back to my unit on a Saturday evening. I was assigned to the 505th Parachute Infantry Regiment, 82nd Airborne Division, a rapid response unit stationed at Fort Bragg, NC. Our Battalion Commander told us we were heading to New Orleans to respond to the devastating Hurricane Katrina. Less than 24 hours later, we were packed, marshaled and heading down to New Orleans on C-17 Air Force Aircraft and Humvee Convoys as well.

Once we arrived in New Orleans, the scene was indescribable. It looked like something out of a "Zombie Movie" or the movie *Escape from New York*. There was no electricity, no people, no traffic, just police guiding traffic through the ravaged, streets. There were generator powered lights on each corner of the French Quarter, which didn't suffer too much flooding, so the roads were drivable. Then we arrived to our compound we were assigned, which was a Naval Reserve Center just outside the 9th Ward District, along the waterway that separated New Orleans from the mainland. They placed us in empty, abandoned offices, within a building that reeked of rotted meat because of the freezer in the dining facility which lost electricity with the rest of the city, and half the state of Louisiana. We entered the building, not knowing what we would find, as we shuffled with our duffle bags and ruck sacks, through the hot, stenched, dark building. We used flashlights attached to our rifles to find our way, like we were back in Iraq searching through a home.

The next morning we ventured out and were assigned certain sectors with vehicles to begin searches for stranded or trapped survivors within the inner-city neighborhoods of the 9th Ward. What we witnessed was indescribable to any human standard in United States. Bodies floating in the flooded streets, abandoned dogs swimming through the brown, bloody water. And not just any type of dog, mostly your average inner-city subculture of owning Pitt-bulls, and Rottweiler's, so the fear of getting bit was also thrown into our new scenario.

As we entered down one street, deeper into the neighborhoods, off the main Boulevard, that's when we first found "Blue". Blue was an approximate 300 pound, African American Corps, lying on top of a small compact car, face down. He didn't have this fictitious name until days later when we realized he hadn't been removed from this horrifying scene. Instead, Blue was still lying on the roof of this car, face down, and sprawled out. As the water receded day after day, we still were ordered to travel down this eerie street that was totally deserted, except for Blue, some dogs, and whatever other corpses remained in the vacant homes. Blue was getting worse, as we were now over 10 days after the hurricane hit, plus it was still averaging 100 degree temperatures. He was rotting away on top of that car, and we noticed that his left hand was now missing. Did it fall off from decay, or did a pit-bull eat it off his arm, we asked ourselves? Green and yellow puss was now running out of Blues head, down the windshield of the car. Needless to say we left the scene and for about the third time, we told a FEMA representative about Blue, and there response was that they were aware of him, but the "Body Recovery Teams" hadn't made it that far down yet. We had a hard time believing that there were any body recovery teams in the entire city yet period, because there were bodies that we discovered against walls in other parts of New Orleans, outside of a Piggly Wiggly's grocery store, in the Superdome, and along I-10 raped up in a black garbage bag.

When it was all said and done, my unit did rescue more than 150 displaced members from the community. The bodies were finally recovered after two weeks of being exposed to the elements. I still remember the spray painted markings on the houses that represented that there was still dead bodies in them, waiting to be recovered.

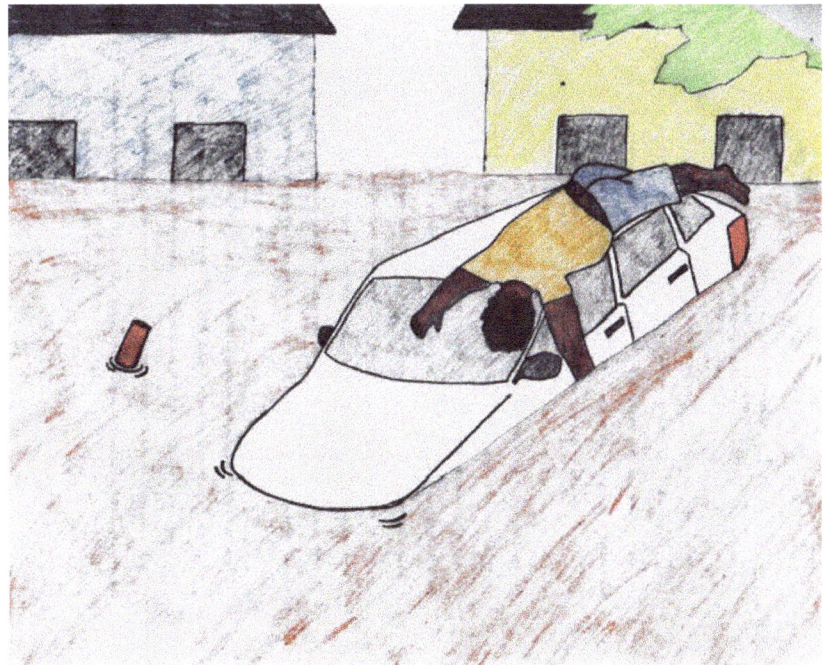

Master Sergeant Nathan Aguinaga, Kuwait, 2008. Just prior to flying up to Baghdad on our year-long and my final deployment to Iraq. Thank you all for reading my stories of my time in the U.S. Army. I would do it all again because this beautiful nation we live in is worth defending and dying for. God Bless the United States of America.

ACKNOWLEDGMENTS

First and foremost, I have to thank my wife Jessica for putting up with my antics at times. Her support for me has been sensational from the time we started dating years ago. She has dealt with my anger issues, lack of patience at times, and of course my bad dreams that occur very regularly. I want to thank her for her chapter she wrote for this book on her experience as a spouse living and dealing with somebody with PTSD. Great job, Jessica!

To my daughter Madyson, thank you for encouraging me and actually convincing me to write this final book of this series on my military experiences and stories. You actually said it was a very important subject that needs to be discussed. As a current college student, you said that it could be used as a tool for some young students that are studying the world of psychology, and I strongly agree.

To my son Taylor who puts up with my impatience, especially when we go out bass fishing. I'm pushy at times, but what father is not? You should have been around my household growing up in the eighties. You have always been very respectful to me and everyone you encounter, and I am so proud of you, son.

To Command Sergeant Major Augustus Pearman. You shaped my life in the military, and made me the senior leader that I became. This man actually "taught me" the 82nd Airborne Division. He taught me how to be a leader in that very difficult military environment—that's a fact.

To all my friends and colleagues in my hometown of North Baltimore, Ohio. Especially to my three great friends Jim, Joe, and John Stewart, who would do anything for me, even after all my "dramatics" at times. Actually, we all have our times of dramatics with one another, and that is what defines true friendship. These three buddies of mine are also officers in our community's fire department and have definitely seen the horrors of death and destruction themselves—sometimes on a monthly and even at times a weekly basis for years. I sometimes wonder what their dreams consist of.

Also, to the police department of North Baltimore. I love you all as well, especially to my colleague and friend I work with at North Baltimore Middle and High School, "Officer Mandy." She knows a lot about the stories I have to tell, as she's been in law enforcement for decades and is one of the most experienced police officers in not only our county, but especially within our community. I feel relieved to serve with someone like her in today's uncertain or crazy world of the unknown that may or may not exist in our education society. I will always have her back, no matter what. I will always have her and every other law enforcement officer's six.

To my friend Dave Bushy from North Baltimore, Ohio, as well. Dave is a Vietnam War veteran who served as a combat medic in an Infantry Battalion. He was wounded by enemy fire and was awarded the Purple Heart. He and I were sitting in the American Legion one morning having breakfast. He said to me, "Nate, write these stories down because you will forget them eventually. You will forget names, places, and even events that happened to you and your units. So write them down." God bless Dave, Ron (Gomer) Stewart, Don Stewart, Jim Wymer, Sam Bretz, my father-in-law Ron Stemnock, my uncle Isidro Aguinaga, who was also a retired Master Sergeant from Fort Bragg, and every other veteran that served over in that jungle in Southeast Asia during that conflict. That generation of warriors was the first to experience an insurgency enemy. I couldn't imagine their dreams. Also, to Gage Stewart, who fought in Afghanistan, and my brother-in-law Ronnie Stemnock, Jr., who fought in Iraq. Actually, Ronnie was at FOB St. Michael also, but about a year after I left. Small Army and small world, isn't it? Also to my buddy Gregg Rockhill, who also fought in Iraq as a combat engineer, clearing those bombs for us. God Bless these friends of mine.

To my good buddy from my hometown of Lapeer, Michigan, Matt Stevens. Matt is a retired Infantryman who served at least four combat deployments in Iraq. To my buddy Neil Casey, who is another Afghanistan veteran. To Ben-Ten Flores & Crystal Carroll, who are both Iraq War veterans. To Kim Kiner, another friend of mine that grew up with my wife Jessica, who's another Army veteran. To my friend Frank Sesok, who was an Army Green Beret during the 1960s and early '70s. To Thomas Lee and Craig Rose, who are also military retirees from my community of North Baltimore, Ohio. To Dougie and Andrea Brim, who are also Air Force veterans and friends of mine. To Danny Buchanan, who was a combat medic in the 173rd Airborne in Vietnam. I never got to meet Danny before I moved here because he passed, but he's a friend of mine's father that served over there, too. To all three of the Meggitt brothers, Dave, Andy, and Kevin. All three served in the Marine Corps. My neighbor, Joe Kipling, also served in the Marines. To Bret Mills, an Army veteran that served in Germany during the heart of the Cold War against the Soviet Union. To my buddy Alex Nichols, who is currently active duty Army. To Officer Devin Lafferty, an Army veteran who is now on a SWAT team. God Bless all these individuals from my community I've lived in since I retired from the service ten years ago.

To John Koehler and the men and women of Koehler Books for all your support and help making these three books possible. Your editing and design process always runs smoothly and without a hitch. Thank you for the opportunity, Mr. Koehler. You gave me a chance for success for my very first book last year, and I truly am appreciative for your confidence in me and of my possible potential.

To all of my friends and family, in person, and on social media. Thank you so much for purchasing and reading my series of books on my time in the military. I hope I could entertain you, make you laugh at times, and simply just interest you in my stories. Your everlasting support means the world to me, and I am forever grateful.

Finally, to all my brothers and sisters that I had the pleasure to serve with in my twenty years in the United States Army and all those that serve in the military today. If you have been diagnosed with having PTSD, that's okay. You're not alone. If you think you have problems sleeping from bad dreams or have road rage, or you sometimes go off on someone, or you simply feel like beating someone's ass at times—get help and talk to someone. It's all good.

www.ingramcontent.com/pod-product-compliance
Lightning Source LLC
Chambersburg PA
CBHW042127100526
44587CB00026B/4197